# TONDERAI:

# STUDYING ABROAD IN ZIMBABWE

## PERRIN ELKIND

Lost Coast Press
≈
Fort Bragg, California

*1998*

Tonderai: Studying Abroad in Zimbabwe
Copyright © 1998 by Perrin Elkind

All rights reserved. This book may not be reproduced in whole or in part, except for passages excerpted for the purposes of review, without prior written permission from the publisher. For information, or to order additional copies, please contact:

Lost Coast Press
155 Cypress Street
Fort Bragg, CA 95437

www.cypresshouse.com
phone (707) 964-9520    fax (707) 964-7531

**Library of Congress Cataloging-in-Publication Data**

Elkind, Perrin, 1973–
    Tonderai : studying abroad in Zimbabwe / Perrin Elkind.
      p. cm.
    ISBN: 1-882897-20-X
    1. Zimbabwe—Description and travel.  2. Zimbabwe—Social life and customs.  3. Elkind, Perrin, 1973– —Journeys—Zimbabwe.  I. Title.
    DT2904.P47   1998
    968.91'051'092–DC21
    [B]                                                          97-48556
                                                                 CIP

Cover by Gopa Design and illustration

Book production by Cypress House

Manufactured in the USA

First Edition

# TONDERAI

For my grandparents:

*Charles Sidney Elkind*
*Vera Freudenheim Elkind*
*Maria Philips Nathanson*
*Milton Norman Nathanson*

# ACKNOWLEDGMENTS

There are three main people who made certain that I wrote this story. The first is Laurie Billington, my Academic Director in Bali, Indonesia, where I studied for a semester following my semester in Zimbabwe. Laurie is the first person who encouraged me to follow my own path and write a story of what I experienced.

The second person is my mom. I probably would never have started writing this story if she had not insisted that I do so, believing that I had something important to say. She also introduced me to the third person responsible for this project.

The third person is Kim Chernin, who guided me through writing simply by listening and understanding what I said. She provided the space for me to find pleasure in writing and in sharing what I wrote. I am certain that I would never have finished the project had she not been there, always open, curious, and ready to listen.

Many others also contributed to this project. Renate Stendhal was among the first to read the original draft. Her ideas were perceptive and helpful. Jane Lewin, my aunt, edited the manuscript and took time to teach me about writing. Dorothy Witt also edited the manuscript, giving me thoughtful suggestions and interesting perspectives. John Sommer, Dean of the School for International Training, helped make my story available to study abroad participants.

My dad gave constant encouragement and served as a sounding board in times of need. Jeanne Chinn, Amy Hayutin, Kitty Moore, Maria Nathanson (my grandmother), and Frances Tobriner all took the time to read the early draft and offered me their insight and encouragement.

Finally, I thank the Zimbabwean people written about in this book for giving me an experience that I could not keep inside.

# FOREWORD

Perrin Elkind shares with us in this book an experience that every American should have: of discovering a world, a part of our world, that has remained too long elusive. Her discovery takes place in Zimbabwe — as far metaphorically as it is alphabetically from America. In a larger sense, however, the world she describes so engagingly, and with such keen insight and sensitivity, is that of an other — an other way of living, of interacting, of viewing life itself. The fact is that as our world becomes ever smaller, ever more interconnected, and ever more oblivious of distinctions between domestic and international issues and concerns, we need to know and understand that other, because it will become more and more us, as well.

Too few Americans have the kind of opportunity that Ms. Elkind sought out with such eagerness and capacity to learn. Although nearly half a million students from other countries attend U.S. universities each year, only some 84,000 Americans study abroad — a startling inequity if one considers the need for the world's lone superpower to understand other cultures and other realities. Of these 84,000, fewer than a quarter go to Third World countries (including neighboring Mexico), and barely two percent go to Africa — even more startling. The so-called Third World is actually two thirds of the world in terms of population relative to that of the economically most developed nations. This imbalance must be corrected not only from a human understanding point of view but also because of our collective self-interest in terms of the political, economic, social, cultural, environmental and security dimensions in which the world's people are truly interdependent.

When I first read the pages that follow, I found myself vividly transported to my own experiences in a Zimbabwe homestay, as well as in living and working in other countries around the world. Nearly 6,500 School for International Training students have joined Perrin Elkind in college Semester Abroad programs in forty-plus countries over the past half-dozen years alone, over 1200 in the current year. Based on their experience, I know that they too will immediately resonate to her vivid descriptions and thoughtful reflections, as will others contemplating a similar experience, whether in reality or vicariously. As with all of us who truly immerse ourselves in other cultures, particularly those so different from our own, Ms. Elkind returned with a new understanding of who she is. This can be a disturbing experience as we are forced to challenge our very sense of self-identity and being, the existence and nature of which may not have been recognized before. Yet it is a necessary part of every citizen's education for life in our interconnected world.

> John G. Sommer
> Dean, Academic Studies Abroad
> School for International Training
> Brattleboro, Vermont

I've Been Writing

And I have to say that it intrigues me
how these words end up here.
I look at the black ink and know
that the letters are art and the words
are memory in poetry, painting
pictures of moments.

I am lying on my bed next to Hannah's
in the hot Harare October
and I can't sleep
for all the thoughts in me looking
for a place to go, a place to stay.

And here they are.
Years and miles
away from their beginnings.
These words are here and the memories
and thoughts are both there and here and still
inside me.

And so it is
that when I look at the page and see
paintings, poetry, the momentary
reality
I am surprised
to have been there
and also
to see it here.

*Perrin L. Elkind*

# TABLE OF CONTENTS

**POSHI** (One): BEGINNING

    I  Preparing: On the Airplane . . . . . . . . 3

    II  Arriving: First Day

    III  Seeing: Mbare Market

    IV  Accepting: Ranche House College

**PIRI** (Two): LIVING WITH THE MANDAZAS

    I  Adjusting: A New Family

**TATU** (Three): SETTLING INTO ZIMBABWE

    I  Observing: Student Life in Harare

    II  Relaxing: Lake Kyle

**CHINA** (Four): LEARNING ABOUT SHONA CULTURE

    I  Respecting: Wachikwa

    II  Participating: Kyandere School

    III  Belonging: Wachikwa II

    IV  Reacting: Phone Call Home

**SHANU** (Five): UNDERSTANDING WOMEN IN ZIMBABWE

    I  Awakening: Issues Facing Women

    II  Learning: Beginning Independent Study

    III  Feeling: Hannah

    IV  Persisting: Baby Dumping: Searching for Answers

    V  Returning: Wachikwa III

    VI  Questioning: Baby Dumping: Finding Clarity

**TANHATU** (Six): ENDING
  I  Relating: Hannah II
  II  Parting: Kyanderes
  III  Resolving: Baby Dumping: Concluding the Project
  IV  Releasing: History of Oppression
  V  Reflecting

# POSHI
(ONE)

# BEGINNING

**Excerpt 1**

# 1  Preparing: On the Airplane

Sometimes I find myself asking, "How did I end up here?" I remember asking myself that while crouching into the freezing wind and making my way across the icy campus where I had chosen to attend college. As the snow whipped against my face, I thought about the warm winters in my home state of California and wondered why I had chosen a college in Massachusetts.

Now, as the airplane bolts down the runway and lifts into the air above New York, the same question comes to mind, "How did I end up here?" My body is wedged into the stiff, narrow seat; my feet are crammed into the space between my carry-on and the seat in front of me. However, physical discomfort is not what is prompting my question. It is the man next to me who has been talking non-stop who has inspired this soul-searching.

On the South African Airlines movie screen, there is an image of the earth with a tiny airplane indicating where we are. Numbers at the bottom of the screen tell how high up we are, how fast we are going, and how long we have been in the air. None of the numbers are registering in my mind as I struggle to find some mental space beside the man next to me.

The middle-aged, white man is from South Africa. When he found out that this is my first trip to Africa, he began talking and hasn't stopped, even for a second. Normally, I would be fascinated to listen to him talk about his country. However, given that this is the beginning of an adventure that I have dreamt about for a year and a half, I would rather sit quietly and appreciate this moment.

I do recognize, however, that he is the one person who has not asked why I want to go to Africa. He is the only person who has not seemed amazed that an American college student would choose to spend a semester studying in Zimbabwe instead of in Europe. When others asked me why I want to go to Africa, it was difficult to answer them. I usually said something like, "Well, I've never been there before." In all of my efforts to come up with an explanation that would make sense to other people, I never questioned my "real" motivations.

The fact is, it never occurred to me to question my motivation for wanting to go to Africa. I simply accepted this compelling desire to go there. Far away places and people always have inspired my curiosity, especially those that are ignored or portrayed negatively by the news media and general public. I am drawn to places that seem different from what is familiar to me and the challenge to make what is different become familiar. This challenge led me to a college across the country from my home.

My motivation to go to Africa also stems from a simple desire to explore the beauty of other places and cultures and to learn lessons that cannot be learned by staying in one place. It is true that part of the reason I want to go to Africa is that I've never been there. No matter how much information I have about a place, it is what I do not know and cannot imagine that inspires me to go there.

This is not the first time I have acted on my desire to go somewhere far away from my familiar world. As a junior in high school, an opportunity arose for students to go to the Soviet Union. I was determined to go on this trip. I wanted to see the "evil empire," and meet the people who had scared the U.S. into building up a monstrous arsenal of nuclear weapons. I could not accept the image of the Soviet Union as an evil place, and I believed that the people there would be no more frightening than my neighbors. Once there, I realized that I never could have predicted the experiences I was having and lessons I was learning. At that point, my need to see things for myself intensified.

As a first-year student at Tufts University, I lived in a large dormitory with people from all over the country and the world. Tufts encourages students to study abroad and I looked forward to spending my junior year outside of the U.S. I was studying French and considered going to France. However, thoughts of a year in France did not excite me. I had been there before and wanted to go somewhere new, someplace that I knew nothing about.

One spring evening, I was talking with someone from my French class. He was a Sophomore and mentioned that he would not be back at Tufts in the fall. When asked where he was going, he responded, "South Africa." All I had needed was the idea and once it was planted in my mind, everything fell into place. I knew that my junior year would be spent in Africa.

Now, the man beside me has engaged the woman to his right in conversation, freeing me to ponder my situation. I look at the movie screen to see where we are in the world. We appear to be close to the U.S., and Africa is not even on the screen. The screen mirrors my mind: I cannot picture Africa. I have no idea what it will be like.

Last semester, I read books by African authors, saw African films, and read up on the political situation, but the images I encountered have not formed into a cohesive set of expectations. The information has only deepened my conviction that what I will experience in Zimbabwe is beyond my imagination. I am on this plane because I want to know what Zimbabwe has in store for me. Once I am there I will know why I came.

# II Arriving: First Day

As I sit in the back seat of the dilapidated taxicab, surrounded by five other students and large backpacks, I am amazed by what I see as we leave the airport and drive through Zimbabwe's capital. Through jet-lag haze, I register yellow fields, red-brown dirt, pale sky and parched trees. Heat radiates from everything.

Men in dark pants and long-sleeved shirts walk slowly across the wide street. They pause to look at this caravan of taxis full of mostly white students. Every person I see is black; although this doesn't surprise me, I notice it. Everything I see confirms my one expectation: the place in which I have just arrived is very different from the place I have just left.

My eyes try to absorb every building, tree, or person we pass, though I don't know the significance of any of it. Thoughts and questions spin into and out of my brain as fast as my eyes move from one object to the next. Grey city buildings a few stories high, signs for "bottle stores," women carrying bundles on their heads. A rush of anticipation spreads through me as we speed through Harare. Though my brain is churning, inside I feel still and patient. I am exactly where I should be and I am ready.

Not even one whole day has passed, and already I am having to force myself to sit still and think, rather than explore. Since the moment I landed in Zimbabwe, I have been so absorbed by everything around me that I have paid no attention to how I feel about any of it. There is too much happening and too much about to happen.

I have just spent hours trying to call my parents. First, I couldn't find a phone. Then, I couldn't find one without at least six people waiting to use it. When I finally had my turn, it didn't work; I couldn't get an operator. So, I went to look for another phone and waited in line to use it. The program director mentioned this morning that because many Zimbabweans don't have phones at home, public telephones are used differently from in the United States. Here, people use them to take care of business, make appointments, and contact family and friends. As a result, the lines tend to move slowly.

After I waited at another phone, the operator said my calling card wouldn't work and then disconnected me. Ready to give up, I turned to walk back to Ranche House College, which is where we are staying this week. There seemed to be buses everywhere, but I decided I would learn my way around better if I walked. To my amazement, almost everyone I passed on the sidewalk smiled at me and said hello; I'd never been in such a friendly city. Unfortunately, I hadn't noticed how far I had walked trying to find a telephone, and it took me a half-hour of walking in the blazing sun to get back.

I asked someone in the Ranche House College office how I could call the United States. Taking pity on me, the woman allowed me to use the office phone "just this once." I spent about fifteen minutes being put on hold and hung up on by the operator. By the time I was finally connected to my parents, I was so hot, tired, and frustrated that I didn't even feel like talking to them. I now understand that while I am in Zimbabwe, I will have no simple, straightforward connection to anyone at home.

It has quickly become clear that Zimbabwe is farther away from what is familiar to me than I had previously imagined. Harare is full of people who smile and greet me as I walk down the street, but there can be no doubt that I am alone. I am part of a group of students from the United States, but in that group I am alone; nobody knows me. I have always felt strong on my own, but then again, I have never truly been on my own.

The identity I brought with me from the United States is filled with the expectations and realities of the people I knew. I have developed my life and identity within the boundaries of my culture's expectations and realities. Now that I have taken that identity outside of the culture and away from the people, I am like an empty shell. I left at home most of what had filled my identity.

All the parts of my U.S. identity have gathered in one corner of my mind, making me feel off-balance, and leaving a great deal of room for me to fill. I need new perspectives, new realities to balance my mind. This time I want to be conscious of what shapes my identity. I want to know what parts of this culture are to become parts of me.

# III  Seeing: Mbare Market

I've been in Harare for two days, and so far I've memorized the names of the two main streets that lead back to Rotten Row: Robert Mugabe Way and Jason Moyo. Rotten Row is where

Ranche House College is located, Robert Mugabe is the president of Zimbabwe, and I don't yet know who Jason Moyo is. I found out that when Zimbabwe gained independence, the new government changed the street names in the main part of Harare. Apparently many of the streets were named for important people in black Zimbabwean history, particularly those who were active in the liberation movement here, or in liberation movements elsewhere. The Post Office is on Julius Nyerere; Nyerere is the former president of Tanzania. I don't recognize more than a couple of the street names. There is a great deal of history for me to learn here.

However, before I can start learning about Zimbabwe's history, I need to figure out my present. As I walk with the group of eighteen students toward "Mbare Musika," the Mbare Market, I am fixated on one word: foreign. Everything I look at or hear or smell is perfectly foreign to me. Everything my senses encounter as I step slowly down this earthen sidewalk is rooted in reasons, practices and norms about which I know and understand nothing. Because I don't understand the roots of my surroundings, I feel as if I am floating. It doesn't feel as if any part of me is touching any part of my surroundings. It's not a bad feeling. It is a foreign feeling.

The group's assignment is to find the Mbare Market and then focus on one of the five senses. I am to focus on "sight" and write in my journal about what I notice. What I notice first is myself. I am in a long, full skirt in shades of turquoise and purple, a blue t-shirt and leather sandals. Silver earrings dangle from my ears, a gold ring and jade bracelet sparkle from my left hand and wrist. I wear a black stopwatch on my right wrist. My brown hair falls loosely down my back. I look like the other fourteen women in my group; all college juniors or seniors on a College Semester Abroad program. We were told that to be "culturally appropriate" we had to wear long skirts. Although our attire may be "appropriate," we do not exactly blend in "culturally."

The Zimbabwean women walking down the unpaved sidewalk wear straight skirts that fall just below their knees, plastic sandals or canvas sneakers without laces, and tattered T-shirts or blouses. The colors of their clothes are a bit faded, and they do not "match" colors and patterns the way people in the West try to do. The varied colors and patterns of each woman's outfit create a bright and spirited landscape of clothing. A woman wearing an orange blouse, a magenta and black skirt, and a maroon knit hat walks beside a woman in a cotton-candy pink blouse, an orange and red skirt, and a white cap.

Nobody wears jewelry and most women have closely cropped hair. Some women wear "head wraps" of brightly printed fabric or knit hats. Some men and women are dressed quite warmly, although I am already hot at nine o'clock in the morning. Everyone I see is fairly short. A little over five feet and three inches tall, I never felt like a giant in the U.S. Here, however, I am about the same height as most of the women I see. None of the men are tall, either. Unfortunately, the height similarity doesn't keep me from standing out among the people here.

A woman is walking toward me. Her straight, grey skirt barely covers her knees, and her pink blouse is ripped along one of the seams. Her white plastic sandals are smudged with dirt and they slap the ground beneath her as she moves along the road. A worn pale-green scarf covers her short hair and she does not swat at the fly that lands just above her forehead.

She watches me as I watch her. As we approach each other, I blurt out, "Masikati," only to realize immediately that "Masikati" is the afternoon greeting, and it is still morning. I can't remember the morning greeting in order to correct myself. She smiles and nods at me, looking me straight in the eye, as we pass each other on the sidewalk.

This is the first time in my life that I have felt like a true outsider. I wonder if I am an intruder, if I should not be here. The people I pass by welcome me with smiles and greetings, welcome this stranger who is walking on their familiar land. Yet in this place where everything is strange to me, I feel strange to myself.

I have never noticed myself so much as I do here. I find myself wondering why I do not look like these people, why I do not dress like them. The answers to those questions may lie partly in books of anthropology, sociology, economics, and politics.

But such answers would not help ground me here. I need to discover who these people are, and locate connections between them and myself. Maybe then I will know whether I am truly strange here.

I enter a large warehouse that I realize is the crafts market. Rows and rows of long tables are crammed into a creaky building. Women and men sit behind tables laden with wood and stone carvings, baskets, pots, and other handmade crafts. There are many vendors selling crafts in similar designs and priced the same. No single table stands out and I wonder if the vendors are able to make much money.

I notice women in old, western-style clothes, who carry themselves in a relaxed manner. The children stay close to the women, who tend to sit in groups. The men move more quickly than the women and children, and they walk around alone. Smaller groups of men sit calmly chatting. The market is noisy, full of people speaking Shona, children's high-pitched energy, and the movement of bodies and goods.

As I walk down the narrow rows of the dimly lit market, each vendor summons me: "Hello," "How are you," "Would you like to buy something?" As I pass them, I am only a couple of feet from them and we look each other in the eye. Even though I find many of the crafts beautiful, I do not want to buy any. I have just arrived in Zimbabwe for a four-month stay. I do not know where I will be moving my backpack over the next months, how much money I will have to spend on such crafts, or what other crafts I will see and like in the future. I would rather wait and buy these crafts just before I leave.

Still I find it difficult to look these people in the eye and tell them I do not want to buy anything. I tell them I think their wares are beautiful, and because I will be in Zimbabwe for a few months, perhaps I will come another time to buy some. I move past them and feel that they do not believe me. Perhaps they look at me as a Western tourist who has a lot of money to spend and simply is not spending it on their hard work and creativity.

A mixture of regret and confusion over how to handle the situation simmers in me. I do not know how to communicate to the vendors that I do respect them and want to support their hard work and creativity, or to let them know that I do not want to be an exploitative tourist, but that I do not yet know how to be something better. Knowing how to speak Shona would help me communicate my interest in the people here. They speak English to me because I am white. I would love to be able to respond in Shona.

In order to observe and learn, I must be patient and accept the discomfort of my ignorance. I must also take time to give the vendors a moment with me, just as I am trying to have a moment with them. This is only my second day here. I walk outside the crafts market and have to close my eyes against the blinding brightness of the midday sun.

Making my way toward the entrance of the low-roofed one-room building that houses the food section of the market, I hear a car behind me. I turn around and see a shiny black car with its engine running and no driver in it. Through the people and dust, I spot the owner of the car. His well-tailored suit and proud stride show him to be the obvious owner. He walks briskly and does not look around as he approaches a woman at her table. When she hands him a package of her wares, he gives her his money. Then he returns to his car and smoothly pulls out of his improvised parking space, paying little heed to the dozens of pedestrians scattering to make room for his automobile.

He is the only man I have seen driving a car at the market and wearing a suit that fits and is in good condition. Although other people move purposefully, they walk slowly. He, however, sped in and out like a whirlwind. Part of what makes me foreign is that I have no way to determine what is "normal."

The tangy aroma of ripe tomatoes hits me before I even walk through the door. This warehouse is as crowded with food as the other was with crafts. Table after table hold heaps of tomatoes, piles of onions and greens, far more ripe fruits and vegetables than there are people in this market. Many of these vegetables must rot; there are too many of them. I see some baskets of grain or flour, and many unfamiliar foods. I buy a couple of oranges from a woman selling what looks like a hundred of them.

At a few tables men sell watches and women sell old clothes. I don't understand why people wear tattered Western fashions rather than clothes made of the beautiful African fabrics. In the corner of the market a man sells traditional herbal medicines, including an aphrodisiac that, he informs me, he sells only to men.

One woman is kneeling with a large, shallow basket in her hands. It contains kernels that remain on the bottom of the basket as she shakes it in a low, quick, circular motion, causing shells from the kernels to fly a couple of inches into the air and then onto the ground, leaving the shelled kernels in the basket. She sees me watching her and greets me. I respond with one of the four Shona words I know. She laughs and asks me where I am from. When I explain that I am a student from the United States, she invites me to come shell the kernels with her. I come over and kneel next to her as she places the basket in my hands. It looks so obvious and simple when I watch her shake the basket. I give it a little shake. The kernels slide to the edge of the basket, and no shells pop off.

I look up at the woman, now sitting in a chair. She smiles and encourages me to try again, more quickly, with a bigger flick of the wrist. I try again. A couple of the kernels almost fall out of the basket, and still no shells pop off. "Again," she says, and tells me to shake the basket in an upward motion as well as outward. Feeling awkward, I try again and am relieved when a few shells pop off. The next time, even more do. I quickly reach my peak performance level, but I feel as though I have engineered a skyscraper.

I finally put the basket down and notice that several other women have been watching me and laughing. They ask me what I came to Zimbabwe to study, how old I am, whether I like Zimbabwe, and a myriad of other questions. They start teaching me Shona words. Although it feels good to be interacting with them, the more words they toss at me, the more I begin to feel dizzy from sensory overload. So many unfamiliar sights, sounds, smells, thoughts, words, questions and images crowd my head that I know it is time for me to leave.

On my way through the narrow rows crowded with milling

bodies, I run into Kelley, another woman from the program. Although we met only a couple of days ago, we have no trouble communicating with each other about our experience in the market. Our shared cultural roots allows our words to flow easily. We both need to find a quiet place to sit and jot notes in our journals. Across the road, buildings cast shade onto the empty walkway beside them. We sit there and pull out our journals. Within seconds, a man approaches us: "Hello! Are you writing a story? I'll tell you a story!" He proceeds to tell us about how his car was stolen recently. I do not know what to think of the man or of his story since I have no way to determine normal behavior here, and I am not confident that my instincts will come to my aid. After commiserating with him, we decide to find another spot for writing.

We walk between the buildings, find a place to sit in the heat of the sun, and take out our journals. Within seconds, we are approached by another man. He sits down near us and says hello, but does not ask any questions. He watches us, and I sense that the questions will soon begin, and we will not have a chance to write at all. As if on cue, he begins to ask us what we are doing and where we are from. A woman casually walks over to us and listens to our responses. Then several curious children scurry up to look at us, our journals, our pens. The man, woman, and older children ask us for our addresses in the United States and want us to write down theirs. They ask Kelley to take pictures of them and send copies later. Then they invite us to come to their homes sometime.

I am bewildered by the attention and by how open and friendly the people seem. I never saw anyone in the United States take such a fervent interest in a couple of foreigners. I don't know how to perceive their curiosity, and I cannot imagine how they are seeing me and Kelley.

Finally, Kelley and I say good-bye and head back toward Ranche House College for a discussion about the Mbare Market. I still have not written anything in my journal. All the thoughts are whirling around in my head with no place to settle themselves. Kelley and I walk separately and, for the most part, silently.

As I walk, I feel my sandaled feet strike the soft dirt and my skirt swish around my legs. My back is sticky with sweat and my hair is knotted into a bun to let my neck cool. I am pondering this morning in Mbare and wondering what I have been seeing not-quite-right and why that is. Have I been seeing things in a particular way because of prejudices, preconceptions? What are my prejudices, my preconceptions? Where did they come from? Why did I accept them? How will I learn to see in a new, fresh way? *Will* I learn to see things more fairly? What would it mean to see things more "fairly"?

What gives value to a particular perspective? What outlook is more important for me here and now? I guess the perspective that I don't yet have is the one to search for. The more ways of seeing I have, though, the less certain I will be of my surroundings and of my own roots and habits.

It can be tempting to see only the surface: the friendly people, the colorful environment, and to be swept away by the excitement of being in a new country where everything seems different. But I'm reminded of the superficial generalizations I heard about Africa when I was in the U.S. I want something more than excitement; I want understanding.

At the market, I didn't feel like an intruder, but maybe I was one. Or maybe was not. Or perhaps the question of whether I was an intruder is less significant than why I would be or would not be. What would make me an intruder, rather than simply an additional, different person? With none of my questions approaching resolution, I take a seat in the cool, quiet classroom.

Our director, Janet, asks us to form groups based on which sense we were assigned to focus on at the market. The four of us who concentrated on "sight" gather in the back of the classroom. After we briefly discuss what we each saw, Janet comes to listen to us. I know that she does not want to participate in our discussion, but I need to ask her a question. I tell her that I noticed everyone was wearing Western clothes and I want to know if the people here covet things from the West. I want to know why more people do not wear clothes made of the colorful Zambian "Java Print" fabric.

Janet informs me that the vivid clothes made of African fabrics in loose, flowing styles are expensive. The embroidery around the neckline and sometimes spreading down the fronts of shirts requires careful and skillful hands. The western clothes, like hand-me-downs from the 1970s, are exactly that. The British were in power then; it was before the revolution, before independence. They used to give their old clothes away, and it is likely that many black Zimbabweans buy them today because they are cheap.

As she speaks, I feel a window opening in my mind, the beginning of a new perspective. Of course, most people want to have new, colorful, comfortable clothes that fit. But the western clothes sold over and over again in bustling marketplaces like Mbare are the cheapest people can find.

When the meeting ends, I retreat to my sparsely furnished dorm room to write. As my thoughts and feelings become words on the page, there is a transitory quality in the way I write: fragments of sentences, brief explanations and descriptions, unfinished thoughts. Unfinished thoughts. My thoughts are only beginning here. I know that what I write today, the questions I have and the answers I accept, will be expanded or replaced or forgotten tomorrow. I turn the page in my journal and look at the blank page in eager anticipation. I can hardly wait to see what fills it tomorrow.

# IV  Accepting: Ranche House College

Even though the overgrown plant gets in the way as I walk down the path, I don't mind it. In fact, I am beginning to like it. Because it is a plant I had never seen before that is abundant in Harare, it reminds me that I am in a foreign land. Every time I walk down the path from the dormitory to the kitchen, I have to duck under this reminder of my new location.

Ranche House College is a small, quiet campus with only a few one- or two-story buildings. For our orientation week, the eighteen of us are staying in the dormitory, two to a room. The rooms are spare, and with tile floors, creaky beds, blank walls, and no other furniture, they don't feel homey at all.

We are rarely in these rooms because our schedule is filled with several hours of language training and lectures every day. The lectures are on health risks, the Shona culture, and other immediately important subjects. In the health lecture, we learn that it's OK to drink the water in Harare but not in rural areas. We also learn that an estimated one in five people in Harare are HIV-positive. The lecturer does not have time to describe the social and cultural factors that contribute to the fast spread of the virus here.

Ranche House College serves meals, but I have yet to wake up for the 7:00 a.m. breakfast. Jet lag, the strain of trying to absorb infinite new information, and late nights spent talking to people in the group have me exhausted. My roommate and I buy bread at a bakery so we can wake up later and still have something to eat. By the time we eat it, the bread is a little dry and we have nothing to put on it. Dry bread is worth an extra half-hour of sleep. What I desperately need is about two days of solid sleep.

I have come to the conclusion that a week of sleep deprivation at Ranche House College is meant to bring home to us the idea that we are no longer in charge of our lives and that our participation in Zimbabwe is more important than our personal comfort or desires. Our days are rigidly scheduled, and it would be entirely inappropriate to skip a scheduled lesson or activity in order to take a nap. Our lecturers and language instructors have a lot of energy and enthusiasm, and they expect the same of us, not to mention that everything they tell us sounds important, and I would hate to miss something crucial. For example, I learn that using the left hand can be offensive. Being left-handed, I find this to be valuable information.

Even that plant hanging over the walkway feels like a lesson in accepting my position in Zimbabwe. If I don't acknowledge and accept the plant's presence but instead continue walking upright, it will hit me in the face. If I acknowledge its presence but decide that it annoys me and push it aside, it will bounce back once I've passed, and maybe some leaves will fall off. If I accept that it is there, and acknowledge that perhaps it belongs where it is, I will duck under it and let it be. I've noticed that most of the students on my program duck under the plant or walk around it. I think we are beginning to comprehend that we now need to live according to a structure and culture different from our own, and that we need to respect them.

# PIRI
## (TWO)

# LIVING WITH THE MANDAZAS

# I  Adjusting: A New Family

The bus is jolting around curves and it shakes my thoughts all over the place. This morning we are moving in with our host families. We will be living in the southern suburbs of Harare, which are inhabited by people of black, Indian, or mixed-race. The northern suburbs are where the whites live. We'll be living in "medium-density" or "high-density" areas; "density" refers to the ratio of people to land in a given area. The whites live in the low-density areas.

Yesterday we drove through the low-density areas of big houses with pools and green lawns. The pools and green lawns were more striking than the houses because Zimbabwe is currently experiencing what may be the worst drought in southern Africa in this century. Right now we are driving though the medium- and high-density areas on our way to our families. Many of the houses are merely shacks. The high-density neighborhoods are bursting at the seams with shacks and people and laundry drying outside. The medium-density area we are driving through now is not quite as crowded; the houses look more stable, and some are painted blue or yellow. Nothing has happened yet, but I sense that something big is beginning.

I was told last night that my family has six children, but some may be older or away at school and not live at home. I will be sharing a bedroom with at least one other person. There may or may not be an indoor bathroom. We had a lecture on Shona culture and family yesterday. According to our lecturer, a

Zimbabwean who teaches at the University of Zimbabwe, the concept of "privacy" is not so revered here as it is in the U.S. With six children and a roommate or two, I may miss privacy.

According to our lecturer, the family structure here is also different from the "nuclear family unit" we are used to in the U.S. Here extended family plays a central role. There is no word for "cousin" in Shona, because all such relations are considered brothers and sisters. In addition, "aunt" and "uncle" are referred to in the same way as "mother" and "father." It will be exciting to learn about the family while being in it rather than from a lecture.

Our director calls out, "Mandaza family!" I look up and realize she is looking at me, that it is my turn to get off the bus. It is time to meet my family. Out the window, I see a young woman, maybe a few years older than I, and a young boy of around ten, standing outside a blue house. I grab my backpack and make my way off the bus.

I sense that what I am embarking on will be a major experience; but after imagining my Zimbabwean family in a million different ways, some good and some a little more challenging, I try not to think about it. I am trying to make this moment fit into some version of "normal" that I constructed over the past week of orientation. I am approaching this moment with the attitude that I came to this country to learn about it from the inside out, that I expected to live with a family, and therefore the fact that I am getting off this bus to go live with a family makes complete sense. I have to laugh at myself as I set my backpack down on the ground. Nothing is "normal." There is no such thing.

The woman in the red-and-black polka-dotted shirt and black-and-white flowered skirt lifts up my backpack and carries it through the gate with no acknowledgment of its excessive weight. As the bus moves away from the curb behind me, I turn and wave at the other students, who are about to be dropped off at their new families as well. Some of the students smile at me, and some simply watch, fear in their eyes. I look back at the woman who has taken my backpack and try to smile at her, but she is looking at the ground.

"Mangwanani," I greet the woman in Shona, "Good morning."

"Mangwanani," she responds. I strain to remember the rest of the morning greeting.

"Marara here?" I ask, "Did you sleep?"

"Ndarara kana mararawo," she says, "I slept if you slept." It's my turn again: "Ndarara," I reply, "I slept."

"Tatenda," she says with a nod, "Thank you."

"Musatenda." "You are welcome."

As we complete the morning greeting, she continues looking at the ground. I wonder why she will not lift her eyes to me. She does not ask me any questions. My image of what it would be like to move into my host family's house was different from this. I imagined our meeting would be more like my experience at the market, that the family members would have a ton of questions for me right away and that I would have a ton of questions for them, too. But right now I feel tongue-tied.

For lack of anything more profound to offer, I tell her, "I'm Perrin," which I know she already knows, and then ask, "What's your name?"

"My name is Hannah." She looks at me for a split second, then back at the ground, her head cocked to one side.

"It is nice to meet you. Thank you for carrying my backpack. It is so heavy!"

"It's OK. It is not heavy."

I wonder if Hannah is my host-Amai, "Mother," or if she is one of the children. The boy has disappeared into the house. I ask Hannah where the rest of the family is. In her soft voice, she informs me that Amai is at a wedding, Baba (Father) is at work, and "the boys" are somewhere else. She says "the boys" are in their twenties. I guess Hannah is my sister.

Inside the front gate, a short pathway leads toward the door past some large bushes and two chairs on a patio. This is 9 Oxford Street; apparently the street-name changes of post-independence Harare have not made it to these suburbs. The front door opens into a living room. The living room holds two worn black vinyl couches, a large old television set, a bookshelf with a radio on it, a picture of Jesus, two calendars courtesy of the local bank, and a wooden table with four chairs around it. I am surprised to be in such a nice home after glimpsing earlier the dilapidated houses in the high-density areas.

Hannah takes me and my backpack through the living room to a short dark hallway. She points to a bathroom that has a cracked bathtub, sink and toilet. I think I see something scurry by my feet. Next to the bathroom, at the end of the hallway is the boys' room. Inside, two bunk beds and a dresser fit with no excess space. The walls are covered with posters of rock groups from the United States, Europe, and Africa. The young boy who greeted me with Hannah is lying on his bed while a Van Halen tape screams from the small tape player on the dresser. This place does not feel very foreign.

Hannah has not introduced me to the boy and he has not introduced himself. "Hi! I'm Perrin, what's your name?" He tells me his name is Robert and follows Hannah and me out of his room. Next to the boys' room is the one I will share with Hannah for the next six weeks. She opens it with a key. I look inside and see two single beds with brightly colored quilts. I tell her how nice they are, and she says that Amai made them. The beds are jammed into the corners of the wall opposite the door. The room is so narrow there is only about a foot of space between the beds and only enough space at the foot of the left bed for the door to open into the room. At the foot of the right bed, my bed, is a small, rickety armoire with Hannah's clothes in it. She has cleared off two shelves on its right side for me to keep my belongings. We stuff my backpack between the armoire and the bed so that half of it fits under the bed. I will have to move some of its contents to the shelves because it is blocking the armoire's door. My large, bright-blue backpack looks out of place in this room. I wonder if that's how I look to Hannah and Robert.

Hannah asks me if I am hungry. Not wanting her to go to trouble, I tell her I've eaten. Without comment, she starts walking back down the dark hall to the kitchen. I sit on my bed and look around the room. Robert is standing in the doorway watching me. I sense that he wants to say something, and I look up at him.

He asks, "Do you go to school?"
"Yes."
"In Zimbabwe?"
"Yes."

He is quiet for a moment and then wonders, "Is your mother in Zimbabwe?"

"No."

A look of confusion or concern sweeps across his face before he asks, somewhat urgently, "Is your father in Zimbabwe?"

"No." At this point, I see more worry, or perhaps even fear, in his eyes.

"Do they know Zimbabwe?"

"I can tell them about it on the telephone and in letters." He does not look relieved by my response.

"Do you have any friends here?"

I am reluctant to admit to Robert that I do not yet have friends here. He seems worried about me and I am sure I will have friends soon, so I tell him, "Yes."

"Is Hannah your friend?"

Hannah could become my friend, so I answer, "Yes."

He nods his head and seems to have resolved whatever his concern was. He disappears into his room, and I decide to go see the kitchen.

The kitchen is more brightly lit than the rest of the house. Aqua colored tiles wrap around the bottom half of the white walls. The floor is tiled green and black; there are an old white refrigerator and an electric stove and oven. There is also a back door that opens onto a yard. I push the door open and step into the warm morning.

In front of me is a narrow concrete path framed by a vegetable garden on one side and a small yellowed lawn on the other. Tomatoes, onions, and greens similar to kale, called "muriwo," grow in the garden. At the end of the short walkway are a chicken coop on the right and a wooden shed on the left. Inside the shed, between the gaps in the warped wood, something is moving. Hannah is still in the kitchen, but I sense that she is paying attention to me, so I call out, "What's in there?"

"That's Naranga."

"Ranga? What does that mean?"

"It's the dog."

"Ranga?"

"*Na*ranga. Means 'ranger.'"

"Oh, *Na*ranga."

I feel foolish because I cannot pronounce the dog's name correctly. It could be nice to have a dog in the family. I don't know why it surprises me that they have a pet; maybe a lot of families have pets. I return to the kitchen and Hannah has finished preparing tea. She asks me, "You like sugar and milk?"

"Actually, I'd like it plain, thank you."

"Black tea?" She makes a face.

"I like it that way!"

Hannah leads me back into the living room and seats me at the wooden table, handing me the tea. She has looked at me several times but still not when I talk to her. She sits with me and sips her tea. The tea is hot and strong. I stop myself from trying to figure out where I am, from trying to tell Hannah a little about myself. I simply look at the ZimBank calendar and at Hannah sipping her sweet tea.

Her back is straight and she sits tall. She is not a tall person, rather petite in fact. Her bare arms show strong muscles, and in her solid stature I see a strong, secure body. However, her eyes still look down at the ground. Her wide, large brown eyes are set above prominent, round cheekbones. Her eyes draw my attention because they are big and because they avoid looking at me.

Her head is cocked slightly to the side, as if one ear hears better than the other. She tilts her head so that one ear or the other is turned toward me. However, she does not seem to favor one ear or have a hearing problem. It occurs to me that she may be looking at me in her own way. She is quiet, speaks softly, moves softly though surely, and keeps her eyes quietly focused on the floor. But in all of her quietness, I think she hears everything. When she does look up at me, her eyes are wide open and she does not blink. I feel that she hears me in the same way that she seems to see me when only her ear is turned my way. I feel calm in her presence, although I have just met her. It is OK that she does not ask me questions, although I wonder what she would like to know. In her quiet alertness, she seems to have many questions for me. I also sense that she may not ask them, but rather will see and hear the answers on her own.

"Thank you for the tea, Hannah."

"You are welcome," she nods, glancing up for a moment.

It seems terribly presumptuous of me, but I can't help thinking that she is happy I'm here.

She stands up gracefully and walks toward the kitchen with our cups. Left alone in the living room, I realize that I have no idea what to do next. I could unpack, but I don't feel ready for that yet. I do not yet feel that I will actually be staying here rather than just having tea and then returning to some other, familiar life. Feeling a little lost, I follow Hannah back into the kitchen.

She is staring out the window above the sink and washing dishes. When I ask if I can help, she hands me a towel so I can dry. In the sink are some pots with food still in them. She empties the food into a bucket and puts it on the doorstep. She walks outside and opens the shed and a black dog, similar to a Labrador, comes bounding out. Although she yells at him to calm down, "Iwe!" ("EEE-way," the familiar form of the "you" pronoun), the dog comes to a screeching stop in the kitchen, barks at me, then dashes back out to the yard before Hannah can yell at him to get out of the kitchen. After a lap or two around the yard, still barking, Naranga tears back toward the kitchen and stops at the bucket. As he chomps on leftovers swimming in water, Hannah and I return to the dishes. I gather they don't feed dogs Purina here.

As we take care of the dishes, I ask Hannah about the family. Robert, a cousin of the Mandazas, is visiting from his boarding school this weekend. Amai works in a "bottle store," a place that sells beer and soft drinks in bottles. Baba is the principal of a primary school. Because Hannah refers to Amai as "Amai Mandaza," and Baba as "Mr. Mandaza," I assume they are not her parents. Some families are able to offer room and board to someone for cooking and cleaning; other families may take in extended family members. I wonder if Hannah is here only for cooking and cleaning.

She tells me about some of the previous students the Mandazas have had stay with them. She speaks fondly of a couple of them and says they write to her. Hannah becomes animated talking about the students. "Donna got A's in Shona. She was very good! She takes me camping in the Eastern Highlands after she finish her school. It was very much fun! I have never been camping before she takes me." Hannah is smiling and her eyes are bright and wide open as she looks at me. The most recent student, Judy, "cried so hard at the airport. She did not want to leave." It relieves me to hear that other students had such a positive experience here, and also that Hannah enjoys sharing her life with students. She wants to show me pictures of the other students later.

I walk over to the tall cupboard to put away a handful of spoons and forks. Opening the door, I almost gasp when I see swarms of cockroaches scurrying over the utensils, plates, and bulk bags of food. Their small brown bodies swarm over the objects, up the walls, near my hands. I drop the utensils into an infested bucket, then quickly shut the door and turn back to Hannah, trying to act nonchalant. I have never seen so many bugs in one place.

Following a few more trips to that cupboard, I finish drying the dishes. Hannah takes me out to the front patio and we sit on the metal chairs facing the road. The sun is hot on my face and I squint as two figures walk toward us. Hannah greets them as they enter the yard. The three speak fast in Shona, while I smile blankly. As the two newcomers move out of the sun, I am able to see them. One is a young woman, the other a younger girl. They both smile broadly at me and nod their heads, greeting me. The older one tells me they are our neighbors and asks if Marcus is home. Apparently Marcus is one of my older brothers. When she hears he is not home, the woman giggles and says she'll have to come back later. I wonder if she is his girlfriend. The three continue talking in Shona. I don't mind being excluded right now; I am exhausted from the effort to communicate, and I find comfort in fading into the background for a moment.

Just as I take a deep breath and settle into my chair, the elder of the pair, Rudo, turns to me and asks, "Would you like to go to church? I am going to church now. Would you like to come?" Our program directors advised us never to turn down an invitation, although I have to admit that church does not sound like an appealing place to be at the moment. The fact is, I am not Christian and have never been to a church service. I am not opposed to seeing one, but right now the idea of religion and lots of people seems overwhelming. I would rather stay here and get to know Hannah a little more.

"Sure! I would be happy to go to church! Thank you for inviting me. Should I change my clothes?"

I have been wearing the same blue skirt and shirt for several days, and they don't fit my image of proper "church clothes." Both Hannah and Rudo assure me that I look nice and do not need to change. I hope they are not simply being polite.

Hannah says she will not join us, so Rudo and I walk out the gate. Two dogs bark at us from across the dusty road as we walk away from the house. Rudo yells at them in Shona to be quiet. I wonder if they will obey English. The street looks different now that I am not on a bus surrounded by other students and my director. Suddenly everything seems more real. Simply walking down the street with someone who lives on the street makes me feel more as if I will actually be living here. Rudo walks casually, swinging her hips a little from side to side. She wears a worn yellow dress with a white collar. Though some of the houses on the street are in better condition than others, most look similar to the Mandazas' house. I like the thought of experiencing life in this neighborhood.

Church is held in a classroom at the local primary school. Rudo tells me that it will be a Seventh Day Adventist service. Even though it may be a common Christian service, it is foreign to me. I enter the classroom behind Rudo and see over her shoulder that there are only about fifteen other people there. The pastor walks over to us and gives me a hearty welcome. He asks what church I belong to in the United States. I admit that I do not belong to one, and he tells me he is happy I "finally" came. The pastor and Rudo introduce me to everyone in the room. Through the flurry of names and questions, I see three small children staring at me from the side of the room. I smile at them when I catch their eyes, but they look away or collapse into giggles. After another fifteen or so people enter the classroom and are introduced to me, the service begins.

Rudo and I sit to the left of the podium, about five rows back. I look at the pastor as he opens his notes and wonder what his sermon will cover. His eyes sweep the room, and his hands grip the sides of the podium. As he begins to speak I lean forward in my chair. His words enter the room, and I slump back in my chair. He is speaking in Shona. I only know the daily greetings in Shona. I cannot believe that I am about to sit through my first church service and will not understand a word of it. Rudo looks at me and smiles, apparently appreciating the sermon thus far. I smile back and settle in for a long daydream. Nobody ever mentioned how long church services last.

I look around the room for something to focus my attention on, and my eyes land on the three children. The tallest of the three, a girl with cropped hair, is staring at me. When I look at her, she looks away. I wonder if she is shy or if my presence bothers her. Suddenly she scurries by and takes the seat directly behind me, pulling it up close to mine. As my thoughts twist through the Shona in my ears, I begin to feel something tugging my hair. I lean forward a little to free my hair from the seat back and then return to my previous position. Within moments, I feel the tugging again. I turn my head slightly and see that all three children are now sitting behind me and reaching for my hair. They don't exactly pull on it but take turns grasping the last couple of inches and running their hands through it.

I have no idea what to do. I am sure everyone can see what is happening. In my mind, it is not proper behavior for a church service. If they are just trying to play with me, pulling away may seem rejecting and be rude. If I don't pull away, I may be encouraging inappropriate behavior. I turn to Rudo and whisper, "Those children are pulling my hair!" She turns to see them and smiles at me, affirming what I have just told her. Then she turns back to the pastor and absorbs herself in the sermon. I gather she is not going to help me.

Soon the children seem to lose interest in my hair and move out of their seats again. I wonder why nobody cares that the children are not sitting still. I thought church was for sitting still. The next thing I know, the tallest girl has dragged a chair up beside me. She sits on the very edge of the seat closest to me and leans practically against me. I am bewildered by her attention and do not know how to react. I look at her, and she still does not smile. I feel like an animal in a zoo. All these people are looking at me, the children are touching me, and I can't speak their language. I try to focus on the sermon and see if I can get the gist of it. It is hard to glean anything from words I don't know in a context I've never before encountered.

My bracelet is pressing into my right wrist, and I see that the girl is poking it with her index finger. She slides her finger off my bracelet so that she is touching my wrist, then presses into my wrist and slides her finger toward my hand. As if suddenly realizing that I am alive and that I know she is touching me, she quickly returns her finger to my bracelet, and then finally puts her hand back in her lap.

I wonder if she is touching me because my skin is white. Before I came here, someone mentioned that I might experience that sort of curiosity. Although it intensifies my feeling of being an animal in a zoo, it does not actually bother me. I understand the curiosity. I am different. I look like a whole different species. I may not be the first white person these people have ever seen, but I may be one of the first whites they have encountered who makes an effort to do things the way they do. In some ways, I appreciate the opportunity to show this girl that I am not totally different from her, that my skin feels the same, that a person can be white and still take part in the activities of the black Zimbabweans. Nonetheless, it is a strange feeling to be so strange to somebody else.

Two hours after the Shona sermon began, Rudo and I are able to leave. First we must say good-bye to all thirty people and agree to come back again. I hope that if I do come back here, it will be after I have learned some Shona. Everyone speaks to me in English, so I assume they realize I do not know their language. I wonder what they think I understood of the sermon. It was exciting to meet some members of the community I will be living in. Everyone was welcoming and appreciative of my effort to participate in their lives.

Rudo walks me back to the Mandazas' house, and I ring the doorbell. I know that I live here now, but I do not have a key and don't feel comfortable simply opening the door if it is unlocked.

I hear Hannah walking across the living room to open the door. When I enter, I see two men on the living room couch facing the television. Hannah does not introduce me to them, so I introduce myself. Their names are Kenneth and Marcus. These are my "brothers." They smile and greet me but do not seem especially interested in my presence. I do not know whether I should sit and watch TV with them, try to talk with them, or leave them alone. I feel more comfortable with Hannah, so I follow her into the kitchen once again. I am sure I will have other opportunities to talk with "the boys," as Hannah refers to these young men, once I understand proper etiquette.

Hannah is preparing dinner and allows me to cut the greens and tomatoes that she has picked from the garden. I lift the knife through the circling flies, and then remember that I need to use my right hand. According to our lecture on Shona family and culture, it is offensive to do anything, especially involving food, with your left hand. Since I am left-handed, this matter is of particular concern to me. After some internal debate over which hand I should use to cut with and which to steady the food with, I decide to cut with my right hand because that feels least natural. I cut very slowly and carefully and manage not to slice my left hand in the process.

Hannah is making *sadza,* the staple food here. It is a mixture of "mealie-meal," like corn meal, and water. It is white and of the consistency of stiff mashed potatoes. The taste is bland and it is usually eaten with meat and vegetables on the side. Hannah is pushing and pulling a large wooden spoon through the bubbling white mixture. The muscles in her arms are contracting, and I see the thick mixture's resistance to the spoon. She covers the pot and begins to cook the vegetables, first stirring the tomatoes and onions together into a thin sauce that she calls "soup," then cooking the greens, muriwo, separately.

Soon she pulls out several plates, fills them with sadza, and puts muriwo in a small space next to the sadza. She pours the soup over the muriwo and part of the sadza. My hunger makes the food appealing. The boys must have heard the plates being filled, because they walk into the kitchen, and each picks a plate off the counter. They don't say a word to Hannah, but they ask me if I have eaten sadza before. When I tell them I tried it once, they laugh and say they hope I like it. It isn't very flavorful, but it is filling. The boys return to the living room, and we follow them with our plates.

They are still in front of the TV, watching what looks to me like a Shona variety show. Robert sits on the floor directly in front of the TV. Hannah and I sit at the table in the back of the room. She leaves for a moment and returns with a Coke for me and water for herself. Cokes are expensive, and I appreciate her generosity. She has also given me a fork, but I learned that people here eat sadza with their hands. I would rather do that. I reach my hand into the grainy mixture and bring it to my mouth. At that moment, Robert stands up and says, "You are eating with your left hand!" He is right. I am eating with my left hand, just after reminding myself not to. I could kick myself.

"I am sorry! I know I am not supposed to! I forgot because I am left-handed. I am really sorry!"

Hannah and Robert laugh and say I do not need to be sorry. They don't mind.

"But you noticed I was eating with my left hand, so it *is* true that I should eat with my right!"

Robert responds, "No, it is OK. You may eat with your left hand. It just is funny."

Hannah adds, "Donna ate with her left hand all the time. She was left-handed, too."

I think Donna was the one who got A's in Shona, so she couldn't have been too poor a student of Zimbabwean customs. Since I still feel ridiculous for having forgotten the one rule I was determined to heed, I switch to eating with my right hand and put my left hand under the table. My right hand is just fine. I don't need my left hand to get food into my mouth. At least I have added some humor to their lives.

After dinner, the boys leave their dishes on the kitchen counter and resume watching TV. Hannah begins to wash the dishes, and I pick up the towel again to help her dry. Each time I walk over to the cupboard, I have to brace myself for the cockroaches. I try to open the door a moment before I have to put something on the shelf to give the roaches time to scurry into hiding. My tactic never works. Each time, I look at hundreds of brown bugs crawling all over everything we eat with and much of what we eat. I cannot imagine getting used to this sight.

It is getting late, and as I stifle a yawn and try to focus on the Shona television show, the front door begins to open. Mr. Mandaza is home. I stand up to meet him as Hannah goes back to the kitchen to take his dinner from the warmer. Mr. Mandaza is about five feet six inches tall, with a significant belly and a big smile.

In his rich, full voice he says, "You are our new student! Welcome. I am Mr. Mandaza."

"It's nice to meet you! I am Perrin."

"Yes. You have met everybody?"

"I have met Hannah, Robert, Marcus, and Kenneth. Amai Mandaza is still not here."

Mr. Mandaza speaks in a lilting rhythm that makes each sentence interesting to listen to, "Amai is at work. How are you finding our home?"

"It is very nice, and Hannah has taken good care of me. Thank you for inviting me to stay with you."

"Oh yes, yes. Have you eaten? I will eat dinner now."

"I have eaten, thank you." I stifle another yawn, but he catches me.

"You are tired? You should sleep now!"

"I am tired, but I would like to meet Amai Mandaza."

"She will be very, very late! You should sleep!"

"If I go to bed, will you tell her I am sorry I missed her and that I look forward to meeting her tomorrow?"

"Yes, I will tell her! Now, you should sleep!"

"OK. It is very nice to meet you. I am very happy to be here. Thank you for having me."

"Oh, yes, you are welcome here!"

"Good night!"

"Yes, good night!"

Mr. Mandaza walks into the kitchen and begins speaking with Hannah in Shona. I wonder if they are talking about me. I go to the bedroom I share with Hannah and pull my backpack a couple of inches out from the bed. There is little room to maneuver, but I finally locate my toiletries and pajamas. I put my pajamas on the shelf of the armoire and head for the bathroom. I am looking forward to a bath. Our director told us to use only a couple of inches of water because of the drought, but any amount of water will be fine with me. It has been a long, hot, tiring day.

When I open the door to the bathroom and turn the light on, I see dozens of cockroaches scurrying into cracks and crevices. The ones in the bath tub and sink cannot find their way out in time to hide. Others on the walls are unfazed by my presence and simply continue their business. My heart sinks. The last thing I want to do is take a bath with cockroaches floating in the water. As I brush my teeth, I send a couple of roaches down the drain. This act of power gives me little satisfaction because hundreds are still crawling throughout the house. When I look into the tub and see several large ones, I give up on the bath. Tomorrow I will deal with bugs in the bathtub, but not tonight. If I were in the United States, I would call an exterminator in the morning, but that does not seem to be the appropriate response in Zimbabwe. It seems to me that I'm simply going to have to live with them.

I return to the bedroom and reach into the armoire for my pajamas. My hand stops mid-reach as I watch a roach making its way over a mound of Hannah's belongings on the next shelf. I guess there will be roaches in my clothes. I pull my pajamas off the shelf and shake them out. Though I find no roaches on them, that gives me little relief. It is only a matter of time. I change my clothes and climb into bed after checking the sheets for cockroaches.

I am too tired to contemplate my new life beyond feeling relieved that the family seems likable, and needing to block out the sight of those cockroaches. So far, being in Zimbabwe has felt a little like riding a roller coaster. I have had virtually no time or space to reflect on events but have had to respond almost instinctively to new situations. I may learn a lot about myself from my spontaneous reactions. Unable to stay awake any longer, I fall asleep in seconds.

Today is Sunday and I have no plans until tomorrow, when I go to school. What on earth will I do today? I am expected to spend the day with my family, but I wonder what that will mean. I hear someone walk by the bedroom door. I wonder who is home. How strange to go straight from being asleep to dealing with new people in a new environment. Sleep is one of the most familiar states my mind and body know. Right at this moment, I would appreciate a "neutral zone" between sleep and being in a strange place.

I didn't dream last night. In fact, I can hardly believe it is already morning. I would not even have woken up if I were not so hot. It must be pretty late for this kind of heat. I roll over and see my watch on the floor beside the bed. It is only a little past eight. Hannah's bed is empty and made. I never heard her come in to bed, and I did not hear her get up this morning.

I stretch myself out of bed and put on a semi-clean skirt and shirt. As I walk past the bathroom looking for whoever might be home, I remember the cockroaches. "Mangwanani!" Hannah calls out the morning greeting to me. I look into the living room and see her on her hands and knees polishing the living room floor. My mind is not yet completely awake, and I cannot seem to recall the morning greeting. She prompts me, and we complete it.

Hannah asks me if I am hungry as she puts down her rag, stands up and heads for the kitchen. I follow her and watch as she makes me two eggs and the same tomato and onion "soup" we had last night, all served over a slice of bread. She leads me into the living room and seats me with my breakfast. She tells me she has already eaten.

"Where is everyone else?" I am hoping to meet Amai Mandaza today.

"I don't know. The boys don't want to go to church, so they are not home. Mr. Mandaza will be back soon. Amai is at work." "Amai is at work again? I didn't meet her! When will she be home?"

"You will meet her tonight. She is home earlier tonight."

The front door slides open and Mr. Mandaza walks in. After we greet each other and I assure him that I am eating well, he asks if I want to go to church. I don't know what to say. I do not want to go to church, but if he is going and wants me to join him, I will.

"I did go to church yesterday with Rudo."

Mr. Mandaza shakes his head, "Our church is different."

"Oh? What church do you go to?"

"United Methodist." It's all the same to me.

"Are you going to church today?"

"Hannah can take you."

"You are not going?"

At this question, he becomes slightly flustered and tells me, "I will go later."

Now I really don't know what to say. I don't need Hannah to take me to church if no one else is going. The two of them are speaking in Shona. When they finish, Mr. Mandaza announces, "It is set. Hannah will take you to church." He leaves the room, leaving me wondering how on earth I got myself into this fix.

This church is at least six times bigger than the classroom that yesterday's service was in. There are also at least two-hundred people here. Hannah and I have found space to sit on the edge of a bench near the back. We do not talk to each other much before the service. I am overwhelmed by the number of people and the commotion. Perhaps Hannah is overwhelmed, too.

This time when the service begins, I am not surprised that it is in Shona. Today, I enjoy listening to the language, although I wish I understood it. Parts of today's service are in English, but I still have trouble understanding the preacher's accent. What I especially enjoy today is the singing. There was no singing yesterday, but today the voices are full and rich, reverberating throughout the church. There must be a large chorus, though I can't see it from my seat. It almost makes me forget the heat and how restless I am after sitting for so long.

Just when the heat and flies become unbearable, the service ends. Hannah leads me through the crowd and we stop just outside the churchyard. I am amazed at how many people are here. I notice many are staring at me, and I catch several conspicuous glances in my direction. I am the only white person out of the hundreds of people here. In the United States, I was never the minority in a large group of people. I am unaccustomed to paying attention to my race, so it continually surprises me to be an object of interest on that account. So far I have only encountered curiosity and openness from the people I meet. If any one of them were to come alone to the United States and be the only black person in a group of hundreds of whites, I wonder what sorts of reaction he or she might receive.

"We will go see Amai Mandaza now," Hannah announces, interrupting my thoughts.

"Does she work near here?"

"Yes, we walk."

I follow Hannah through the crowd to the road. We move slowly down the dirt sidewalk, and I find myself constantly thinking of questions to ask Hannah. I decide simply to pay attention to my surroundings now and ask questions later. As eager as I am to know the meaning of everything I see, I want to proceed at a slower pace so that I can absorb the details. I will have plenty of time with Hannah, and I do not want to fill my mind with hasty conclusions.

Hannah leads me into a bottle shop, which is set up like a bar and sells only bottled drinks, such as beer, Coca-Cola, or Fanta. Hannah explains that the "bartender" usually removes the bottle cap before handing the customer a drink. The customer then finishes the drink in the shop and returns the bottle before leaving. If a customer wants to take a bottle out of the shop, s/he must pay extra money as a deposit.

The shop is dark inside and contains only a rickety wooden

bar and a refrigerator. This is where Amai Mandaza works. She is a short, heavy-set woman, and her hair is pulled tightly away from her head into a small knot. She is serving her five male customers beer and does not see Hannah and me behind them. As we step around to the side of the bar, she turns, smiles and comes over to hug me. "How are you finding Zimbabwe?" she asks.

"It is very nice. Thank you for having me stay in your home," I respond.

Before she can say anything, two of the men begin firing questions at me, the other asks her for another beer. I converse with the men for a few minutes while Amai serves beer to her customers, and Hannah tells Amai Mandaza that we are leaving. Although I do not feel that I've had a long enough meeting with Amai, it is clear that now is not an appropriate time. She waves good-bye to me and says she will see me later.

As Hannah and I step outside the dark shop into the sunlight, she asks me if I would like to go to town.

"Sure!" I'd love to be shown Harare by someone who lives here. "Should we take a bus?"

"We will take an E.T."

"E.T.? What's that?" Certainly not the E.T. I'm thinking of.

"You will see."

I soon find myself in the far back of an old Peugeot station wagon with four other people. This is an E.T., an "Emergency Taxi." My back is against the left window and my legs stretch out in front of me. My left side is pressed against the back seat. Another woman sits opposite me, with her legs stretched out toward me against my legs. A man sits opposite her and next to me in the same position and another opposite him. The man closest to the back door does not seem alarmed by the fact that the door he is leaning against is attached to the car with wire and duct tape.

Hannah is one of seven fully grown adults in the back seat. Two women and five men fit into the space like mismatched puzzle pieces. By ignoring the physical limitations of the car, they force it to accommodate them. Two kneel in the small space between the edge of the back seat and the back of the front seats, and the other five work their way around each other and the two on the floor. In the front passenger seat, there are two people. Fortunately, there is only one person in the driver's seat.

No one seems fazed by the fact that fourteen people are riding in a five-passenger car that looks, sounds, and feels as if it is ready to quit before we even get inside. A vague image of a seatbelt and an air bag flits through my mind and then disappears as we screech to a stop and the three bodies to my right pin me against the seatback to my left. At least the car can stop. Hannah hands the driver a dollar (U.S. $0.20) and instructs me to do the same. Everyone piles out of the car so Hannah and I can disembark, and then they all climb back in to complete the rest of their own harrowing journey.

Harare is quiet today. There is little traffic and few people. Most of the businesses are closed. Hannah and I walk slowly up and down the streets and look in the store windows. She tells me that she does not come here often. When I ask what she normally does on weekends, she says she does housework.

As we walk up Jason Moyo Street, we pass a single open business, the Sunflower Bakery. I bought a loaf of bread here a couple of days ago and loved it. All the bread is freshly baked and inexpensive, though Hannah says the price keeps rising because of the new Economic Structural Adjustment Program (ESAP) that the government adopted under pressure from the World Bank and other western influences.

We look in the display shelf at the various scones and rolls. Hannah points at a sheet of yellow muffins and tells me they are "Queen Cakes." A name they must have acquired during the colonial period. I buy us each a Queen Cake and a SunSplash orange juice. We walk outside with our snack and as there are no benches, we sit on the curb. If it were a weekday, we would be run over by buses, taxis, E.T.'s, and pedestrians, but today we can relax and enjoy our snack.

The orange juice comes in small plastic bottles with straws to poke through the top. Each of our straws break before we can poke it through, so I have to cut the top off each bottle with my pocket knife. Once we are settled with our drinks and Queen Cakes in our laps, we begin to chat about the day. We discuss the church and how many people there were. She tells me that the boys in the Mandaza family never go to church; they always make up excuses to avoid it. Then she tells me that Mr. Mandaza doesn't usually go, either. I am surprised because when he spoke to me about church, he made it seem as if he regularly attends. I tell her that in the United States I know many people who avoid church, too. That makes her laugh, and she seems surprised.

I am enjoying sitting on this sunny curb in Harare, nibbling on my sweet muffin, sipping juice, and talking with Hannah. She does not seem to mind taking me around with her, and that makes me feel that my presence here is normal. It is easy to be with her because of her openness. She still does not always look at me, but I believe that she is shy.

"What time is it?" Hannah asks me.

"2:25 p.m."

"Oh my God! I *don't* want to go home and make dinner! I am tired!" Hannah speaks rhythmically and emphatically.

She explains to me that men in Zimbabwe do not help the women with housework:

"They just watch TV! They think cooking is a job just for women! They will starve before they will cook! Is it the same in the United States?"

I tell her that many men in the U.S. seem to think that way, but the more progressive way of thinking is that men should share housework. I tell her that many families try to be more fair than they used to be about household responsibilities, but that generally, women still shoulder most of the burden. When she asks me how a family might share the housework, I give an example of my father's washing dinner dishes after my mother has cooked.

"Oh my God! I *don't* believe it!"

However, from the way she quietly nods her agreement with the idea of gender equality in the home, I sense that these thoughts are not totally new to her. She has probably considered similar concepts on her own.

As we begin walking toward the bus stop to go home, I silently marvel at our conversation. Before I came here, I worried about the sexism I expected to experience. At worst, encouraged by western stereotypes of Africa, I imagined men and women sharing a belief in women's inferiority and not questioning it. Aware that my only concept of sexism in Africa came from stereotypes, I was curious and wanted to learn about the issue from the perspectives of people here. I am amazed that in the first weekend of my homestay, I have found someone with whom I can discuss the issues openly.

I reflect on my surprise when Hannah voiced her dissatisfaction with the "woman's role" here. In the United States, people often trivialize sexist oppression in developing nations by attributing it to "tradition" or "custom." When people accept or even glorify sexism based on tradition, they disparage the significance of the sexism to the women involved. In addition, I see no evidence that cultures and cultural traditions cannot change. "Tradition" is far more dynamic than most people acknowledge. In the United States, it was always difficult for me to accept sexism in developing countries on the ground that "that's just the way they are over there!" Yet I heard that attitude expressed by teachers, friends, and politicians time and time again.

Of course, it is disturbing that equal rights for women in Zimbabwe are far from won, but it feels good to hear Hannah discuss gender inequality with some amount of self-respect and thoughtfulness. I think Hannah will teach me a great deal while I am here. I watch her sitting tall in her bus seat, looking out the window in her quiet, alert way. She looks strong and full of thought. How right it feels to be here in Harare, Zimbabwe, on this Sunday in September. There is no other place I could possibly want to be.

# TATU
(THREE)

# SETTLING INTO ZIMBABWE

# I  Observing: Student Life in Harare

I have been here only for a few weeks, but I think time is passing me by. I cannot remember everything that happens from day to day. I feel that a lot of time passes without my noticing it. This is not like travel, when every minute includes something to take a picture of, something to record in a letter or journal. I have a routine here, and I see many of the same sights each day. Eventually I will travel around the country and visit tourist attractions. For now, I am beginning to live here, and in many ways this is more exciting than traveling.

The sights I see each day are not monuments, old churches, or grand performances. I see people living their lives in a place very different from my home in the United States. I have even stopped noticing every woman who walks by carrying a huge bundle on her head. I don't notice everything that happens in a day because much of it is normal to me now.

Now that I am not surprised by everything I see, I am able to listen, learn, and absorb more about the culture. Each day the other students and I attend a lecture from 9:00 to 11:00 a.m. The time schedule, of course, is approximate. Nothing is as precise here as in the United States. We do not have a regular teacher. Our lecturers are Zimbabweans who come to speak to us about their particular area of expertise and experience.

This week we had lectures on literature and society by two Zimbabweans, one a prominent writer and the other a well-known film maker. Both of them talked about oral literature, or "orature." I enjoyed the discussion of storytelling as an art form so much that I found two books on the subject published by a Zimbabwean press, and I have been reading them in my spare time. It is this kind of time that I do not always notice or recall. Yet it is in such times of quietly gathering information that I begin to form the foundations of understanding that link me to Zimbabwe and its people.

I learned from the lectures and my reading that the oral tradition forms the basis of African literature and is the means by which its people learn and entertain others. Unlike in written literature, in oral literature the performance is crucial to its meaning. In this respect, orature is like music and dance. The performer's facial expression, voice inflection, and movement all affect the message conveyed to the audience.

Intensifying the significance of the performer, many African languages are tonal in nature. For example, the Shona verb "to be" ("ri") uses a special high tone to indicate the third person and plurals. So a story told in Shona might have clearer meanings than when written, simply because of the tonal indicators. I also learn that what is now often considered poetry in African orature is designed to be performed in a musical setting. Many stories in the oral tradition are like operas in the way they combine words, music, and dance.

I like the idea that in the oral tradition the audience is an important part of the story and is expected to participate. For example, the audience might be called on to sing a chorus at certain points in a story. Most African poems and many folk tales include a choral verse for the purpose of involving the audience. It occurs to me that in using orature for educational purposes, the storyteller encourages members of the audience to be active learners, to take an active part in their education.

The mere presence of an audience has the potential to influence the story itself. Depending on the age or gender of the audience, for example, a performer might alter a story's plot or meaning. I imagine how this practice might play a part in socializing young people and orienting them to their culture. A story can grow and change as the children mature, indicating that there is much to explore and learn as they grow older.

Orature expresses the reality that the story of life is always changing and evolving.

In learning from Zimbabweans about their oral tradition, one thing I find fascinating is how different the tradition is from the picture of it that I encountered in the U.S. My teachers in the U.S. gave me the impression that the oral stories were handed down verbatim. However, I am learning that the African oral tradition has no concept of an "authentic" version of a story. Each performer and each new audience are virtually expected to relay and interpret the story in personal, individual ways. I once read an African oral story in the U.S. that was cited as the "original." Now I realize that the citation stands outside the tradition, which does not date and define versions in that sense.

Just as there is no "authentic" or "original" version of a story, so there is no single author. In African orature, each performer's personal truth shapes the story. Each individual is important, introducing something unique that is accepted as a part of the story. As the experience and imagination of each storyteller meld into the others', the group mind becomes the author.

After our morning lecture, we have a two-hour break for lunch. Usually our lectures are given at Ranche House College in Harare, a short walk from the center of town. Sometimes I stop at the Sunflower Bakery and buy freshly baked bread. At other times I buy mangoes or green bananas from men who sell them from cardboard boxes on the sidewalk. The fruit is sweeter than any I'd tasted before coming to Zimbabwe. A lot of fruit is sold on the street, and it costs next to nothing. I wonder how much profit the men actually make from their sales. I have yet to learn how to eat a mango while walking without creating a river of juice down my hands and arms.

On other days, I stop at a "fast food" stand and buy a samosa, an Indian pastry filed with spicy vegetables or meat. There is a significant Indian population here. Indians run many businesses, including fabric stores and food stands. The fabric stores have a wonderful aroma because they also often sell Indian spices. I have noticed some tension between Indians and black Zimbabweans. During colonialism, both sections of the population were discriminated against by the whites. I think that the Indians and blacks may have had to compete for whatever good was available to them, such as jobs or housing. I get the feeling that the Indians are somewhat more financially successful than the blacks.

One Indian storekeeper whom I encountered several times was not always polite to the black Zimbabweans who work or shop in the store, although he was always polite to me. One time I told him that his treatment of the blacks made me not want to buy anything from him. His manner toward me turned cool after that, but didn't improve toward others.

Not all the Indian storekeepers I've met are like him. One woman in a leather shop saved me from being pick-pocketed by a couple of local thieves. Being new to this country, I make observations much faster than I acquire explanations. I am careful to note my questions and opinions about what I see, and I try to ask others for their explanations. I don't know the unpleasant storekeeper's history. I don't know if there are racism and tension between Indians and blacks. In fact I may never know. I find that so many questions come to mind throughout a day that I never have time to ask all of them. Many more will probably arise over the next months of living here.

After lunch, we have Shona language class until 4:30 p.m., with a half-hour break around three o'clock. At the break, Ranche House College kitchen staff serve us tea. Sometimes I forget to ask for black tea and they give it to me with milk and a lot of sugar. On good days, they also serve cookies or crackers for a snack.

The Shona language is one of the biggest stretches my mind has to make. None of the vocabulary words relates to any word I know from English or French. There is no logical reason in my mind for "huku" to mean "chicken", or "sekai" to be the verb for "laugh." My ability to learn this language is dependent on my imagination to accept these new words.

Of course, there is no real reason in my mind for any of the words I know in English or French, but I have grown accustomed to their sound. Though I have never heard a language that sounds like Shona, I like it. It sounds musical, the way the vowels are drawn out and the syllables enunciated almost rhythmically. I also like it because it is different from the Romance languages to which I have been exposed. Since language is a part of culture, I am stretching my imagination to draw me closer to the culture.

However, the truth is that nobody in Harare speaks Shona to me. They see that I am white, so they speak English. If I respond in Shona they may speak a bit of Shona with me, but once I fumble for a word they return to English. Everyone in Harare seems to speak English better than I speak Shona. English is still one of Zimbabwe's national languages, and it is taught in schools. So I do not get to practice Shona very much.

By the time classes are over for the day, I am exhausted. At my college in the U.S., I looked forward to going home after a long day. Going home meant relaxing with people like me and being separate from what I did during the day. Here, however, going home is a continuation of my daytime efforts to learn about Zimbabwe. There is no time when I am not "on": alert, trying hard to understand, and to be understood.

Even the bus ride home frequently involves a conversation with someone about what I am doing in Harare and why I am on a bus to Southerton (since whites don't live in Southerton). From the moment I wake up in the morning until I go to bed at night, I am alert and aware. Every conversation involves explaining or asking questions about the simplest and the most complex matters.

I cannot become frustrated with the next person who asks me what I am doing in Zimbabwe, even though fifteen people may have asked me the same question today. I cannot appear bored when I answer the next person, and the conversation that ensues is identical to the other fifteen I had. And I cannot reveal impatience when I am unable to locate my bus and when the person I ask for directions has to ask five other people their opinions on the best bus for me to take, then becomes involved in conversations with those people. I do not know where my bus is, and until I figure that out, I am dependent on others.

I am constantly aware that I am a guest wherever I go in this country and that misunderstandings between cultures or races often stem from people not listening, not talking. So I feel a responsibility to listen and talk. Frankly, being "on" all the time makes me tired. Although I am excited by all there is to learn and by many of the people I meet, my energy has no time to replenish itself because I never stop using it.

Last weekend I decided to spend a day at the Zimbabwe National Gallery. I thought that a quiet day looking at art would be relaxing. And at first, it was. I was fascinated by the huge costumes for dances in Liberia. They were made of natural materials, some were painted with bright red and white designs, and some looked sort of like animals. There was a wooden stool from Liberia, called a "man's stool," which had as its stand a kneeling woman. What the kneeling woman carried on her head formed the seat.

The day ceased to be relaxing when I began to think about the art, and about the fact that the costumes are now in an art gallery. I wondered how much the traditions and dances are still an important part of life in Liberia. I thought about the influence of colonizers all over Africa. I then began to ponder the implications of a "man's stool" as an artifact on which a man could sit on a kneeling woman. Or is the kneeling woman supporting him with all of her strength? Who made this stool? Finally I began to notice that none of the art work in the permanent collection was made in Zimbabwe. Why is there no Zimbabwean art work in its National Gallery?

Before I left the gallery, I walked upstairs to see the temporary collection. This month, the temporary collection happened to be from Zimbabwe. I entered the room and instantly felt a calm wash over me. Facing me were Zimbabwean stone carvings. These large blocks of stone, some black, some green or brown, had been transformed by imagination and skill into abstract shapes of people, emotions, gods, history. This art spoke to me not as stone but as thought and feeling. The stillness of the thought and feeling is the calm I felt.

One black carving, two feet high, was a rounded figure holding another rounded figure within. Although it was abstract, it appeared to be a woman holding a baby. The woman's head was a circle held down between her rounded shoulders. The baby was another circle, held where folds of stone indicated arms coming together. The feeling expressed through cold stone could not have been conveyed more clearly in a representational carving. The abstract depiction matched the inexplicable emotion the carving gave me.

The art in the Zimbabwe National Gallery affected me differently from the way a collection of Monet paintings would. These exhibits left me curious, thoughtful. I have so many questions about the people here, about this country, and this continent. My relaxing day at the art gallery did not turn out as I'd expected. As time goes on, I think I will have many more experiences like this one.

Some of the students from my program have started going to a local bar after school before going home. Today I am joining them, feeling a need to relax between school and home. We are in the bar at Queen's Hotel, and I immediately notice that it is full of men. In my program are four men and fourteen women. Three of the men are here and six of the women. We are the only six women in the bar. Later a few more women will come. They are prostitutes. Other Zimbabwean women are at home cooking for their families.

A week ago, I might not have chosen to come to this bar, thinking it was more appropriate for me to go straight home from school. This week I feel differently. Since I moved into the Mandazas' house, the basic structure of my life has been stable. I see my perspective evolve within the unchanging frame of my life here.

Although it is important to me to be as "culturally appropriate" as possible, I cannot become Zimbabwean. Gradually, I have come to realize that I can trust myself to understand what is truly offensive to the people here. I can relax. It is not inappropriate to adhere to norms of my own culture, as long as I am respectful of this culture. For example, I feel comfortable going to the bar this evening even though I know that if Hannah were a student, she would definitely go straight home. The fact is, it often seems that I appear strange, whether I am doing something exactly as a Zimbabwean woman would or something that only a western woman would.

Before I felt comfortable blatantly doing something as "strange" as going to a bar after school, I needed to establish a connection with the Mandaza family. After having spent time with them in their home, I feel that they grasp my commitment to learn about them and their culture. It has taken time to develop a relationship; even last week I might not have felt comfortable coming to this bar instead of going straight home.

A week here is a long time because every moment is packed with learning. The Mandazas and I have been developing an understanding. I make an effort to ask questions and participate in their culture; they accept our cultural differences and tend to laugh at the weird things I do. It is comfortable to be relaxing and laughing at our differences rather than feeling as if I should always try to behave like a Zimbabwean.

As the men watch us walk through the bar, I see that we are the only white people here. I imagine the "Rhodies" have their own bars. "Rhodie" is the term for the white Zimbabweans who opposed Zimbabwe's independence and majority (black) rule. Those whites still consider themselves Rhodesians, even though Rhodesia became Zimbabwe in 1980.

We take our seats around a low table and decide what we want to drink. None of us drinks very much. It is not the alcohol we are here for but the space to let our minds relax. As I go to the bar to order, a man swivels around on his stool to face me.

"Hello," he says.

"Hello," I respond. I do not want to talk to this man.

"You will marry me," he announces.

"Excuse me?"

"You will marry me."

"No I will not. Bartender, I would like two Castles and one Zambezi, please."

"You will marry me. Do not worry."

Worry is the last thing he inspires. Irritation is the more accurate term. I take the drinks and return to the corner of the room where the rest of the students are gathered. I could have told the man at the bar that Rick, Adam, or Mike is my husband. Most of the women in my program have done that. I don't want to bother. Anyway, the regular patrons might start to notice that these three young men have several different wives.

The bar is dimly lit. Our group sits in a circle around a low, square table. Although it was not our intention, the circle allows us to see only each other. My back is to the bar and I face the students and the window. As I sit back in my chair, I feel my mind settling down. I do not have to listen carefully or explain anything right now. So far we are not a close group. All that matters is that we come from the United States and are students here.

I stay for an hour and then decide to head home so that I am not late for dinner. As I walk to the bus station, the sky begins to darken into dusk.

"Are you an American student at Ranche House College?" I hear a voice from behind me. I turn to see a man with dreadlocks topped by a rainbow knit hat. He smiles broadly from behind a moustache and beard. I have no idea who he is.

"Yes...Who are you?"

"I am Cris. I am a musician. I study Ethnomusicology." There is a College of Ethnomusicology near Ranche House College. We have met some of the students there, and they have been friendly to us. Cris has a bright smile and an easy manner that make me want to talk to him. He tells me that he plays drums and mbira, the thumb piano. When I ask if he will teach me to play drums, he smiles widely, his teeth glinting, "Yes, of course!" He is a student of Ephat Mujuru, a well-known mbira player and drummer. We have heard Ephat's band in Queen's Garden several times. They play beautiful music.

The hot day has cooled off into a typical Harare evening. People move more slowly and the sidewalks empty as the buses fill with passengers. The sun sinks behind buildings, and the dusky light settles in over the city. I'm enjoying standing on the sidewalk chatting with Cris and watching people walk by.

It has become usual for me to spend time talking with random people on the street. Men and also some women don't hesitate to approach me, even just for a bit of friendly small talk. At first the openness surprised me because I was accustomed to cities in the U.S. where people try to keep to themselves. Now I appreciate the casual friendliness, unless I am in a hurry. Because Zimbabweans don't hurry with the intensity of a Westerner like me, they don't always seem to understand when I say I have to leave. Still, it is a lesson in cultural differences.

Cris and I reach the bus terminal, and he says goodbye with a nod of his head and a big smile. On the ride home, I wonder why it feels so natural for the other students and me to become friends with the musicians. Hannah and I get along very well, but our positions in life are so different. These musicians live an independent lifestyle, having made a choice to study and play music. They have hopes and dreams of becoming famous and they are working toward that. I do not know if Hannah sees choices for herself that could move her any closer toward her hopes and dreams. All of the musicians we have met have been men. I wonder if a woman here would have the opportunity to choose the same lifestyle these men have.

I arrive home as the sky turns to black. I take a deep breath, shifting out of my hazy, introspective mode, and focus on 9 Oxford Street. The time at the bar was exactly what I needed: a little space between learning at school and learning at home. As usual, Naranga flies at me from the yard when I open the gate. "Iwe," Hannah admonishes him from the kitchen and pokes her head out the door to smile at me. I am just in time for dinner. I know the rest of the evening will include doing dishes, talking with Hannah, doing Shona homework, reading articles for tomorrow's lecture, and going to bed. If Baba is home, I will talk with him about something happening in the news in Zimbabwe or today's lecture.

Time here is swollen with experience. Sometimes a day passes so quickly that I hardly notice it. But when I reflect on this day, I see layers of experience that have occurred at each moment. There are many more layers that I cannot see, but can only feel.

My identity in Zimbabwe clarifies with each day as I interact with people and continue to learn about my surroundings. As my understanding of the Shona culture deepens, I also learn more about my own cultural background. I am sorting through different aspects of where I come from and where I am now and finding threads within myself to weave into the two locations.

In many ways, my activities here are the same as they would be anywhere. Go to school, go out with friends, meet people, and think a lot. This is hardly different from the life I established at college. Here, as at college, I do not remember everything that happens in a day because much of what I am learning is subtle. Each observation is a small seed. As time passes, the seeds open. In time I may find a rich field spread out before me. I imagine the field to be endless.

# II  Relaxing: Lake Kyle

Alone on a ridge above Lake Kyle, I hear noises in the trees and brush surrounding me. The rock I am sitting on is cool and flat, as if it exists solely for someone who wants to relax quietly in these woods and write in her journal. Dry, sharp grass and leaves prick my feet between the straps of my sandals.

After almost a month in Harare, I am on a short journey with the other students to see some sights beyond the city. A rickety and crowded van carried us on bumpy roads through rural land to deposit us at this tourist destination. We are the only people here. I find it interesting to be a tourist, yet feel a deeper connection to the landscape than I would as a mere sightseer.

Now that I feel grounded in Harare, it is time to expand my scope and look outside the city, outside what I have seen and learned there. Each new place I see adds a strand to the web of connection I feel between myself and Zimbabwe. It is exciting to watch the web grow more complex.

Below me is the lake, the second-largest body of water in Zimbabwe. Earlier as I walked down to the water, I had to cross over cracked earth that before the drought was covered by water many meters deep. The landscape is a scene of suffering: dry earth, parched trees, thirsty animals. Somebody told me that this area used to be lush, a rich and thriving forest. The colors now are shades of grey and brown. Although in its drama and spaciousness, this land is still beautiful, the signs of death are haunting.

In the shade of these trees I am cool, and my body relaxes against the smooth rock. However, inside I feel restless, but it is a feeling I have grown accustomed to, knowing there is no way to avoid it. The restlessness arises the moment I realize that I am in a beautiful place or with wonderful people or am learning something special. It surfaces the moment I remember that beneath the beauty and wonder of my experience, there is deep suffering.

When I see the cracked earth on the reservoir bed, I cannot ignore the effect of the drought. Electricity is rationed in cities, cattle are dying, wells are drying out, crops have no chance to flourish, unemployment is high. I have seen the poverty at a formerly successful cooperative farm that is now barely able to feed its members. The loss of pride and self-respect that come from providing for oneself may be as devastating as hunger and the fear of what is to come if the drought continues.

I marvel at the beauty of the landscape before me and am warmed by thoughts of the generous people who have served me sadza and offered tea. But underneath my appreciation of this beauty is a personal suffering that comes from knowing the misfortune of those around me. My restlessness is the result of my position in Zimbabwe.

On the one hand, I am a participant in the lives of the Zimbabweans with whom I live or have friendships. I witness their daily struggle against increasing odds. On the other hand, I am only a visitor and have no active role in the struggle. I am neither a victim nor a perpetrator. I am a witness who does not affect the situation but merely acknowledges that it exists.

By nature, I am not cut out to be a passive witness. I want to affect a situation once I decide something is wrong. In Zimbabwe, however, my impulse has a long way to go before it can be transformed into action.

First, deciding what is wrong takes time, inquiry, and thought on a scale far greater than would be required of me in the United States. Here the economic, cultural, and governmental systems are foreign to me, and their subtle interactions are not always easy to discern. Although I am aware of the severity of problems and understand the basic causes, there are many dimensions I do not see. Without knowing the intricacies of the issues that surround my life in Zimbabwe, I am helpless to know where I can have an impact.

I hear a rustling in the bushes and trees that seems to be coming closer to where I sit. The noise has been constant since I first sat down, but when I look up I see nothing. It sounds like footsteps, like a person lurking in the bushes. Strangely, this sound does not scare me, but just makes me curious.

I have no idea why I am not frightened. All I know is that the whole time I have been in Zimbabwe, I have had to rely on my instincts, and they have not failed me yet. Because I lack information about everything that occurs here, I cannot base my decisions on fact alone. More and more, I find myself trusting my instincts when it comes to topics of conversation, behavior, and even the unpredictable bus schedules.

Mainly I rely on my instincts when deciding whether to offer an opinion if I think it might offend someone. Sometimes I choose not to comment on one of Baba Mandaza's sexist remarks, a decision that does not mean that I have given up trying to broaden his view of women. Rather, I have acquired a new sense of when to say something and when to wait. In the United States, I never hesitated to state my opinion. Because this is a different culture, and because I wish to create an atmosphere of respect, I need to be sensitive to others. Once respect and trust are established, Baba Mandaza and others may be more willing to listen to me. So I follow my instincts and hope they lead me where I am trying to go.

I think that the restlessness I feel in wanting to affect the suffering in Zimbabwe is inevitable. My instincts tell me to wait, that I will know when to say something, when to do something. I need to trust myself, let my instincts tell me: "Now is the time." My restlessness comes from my impulse to change a bad situation into something better. My Western take-charge mentality conflicts with my position here. I am a witness. I know I must wait my turn to speak, but that turn will come.

I close my journal and look around. What is causing that rustling? I hear it right behind me and whirl around. I see nothing but a tree. Footsteps, then rustling in a bush just three meters from me. Now a stir in the tree next to the bush. There he is: a grey monkey with a black face, less than two feet tall, staring at me from his perch on a branch halfway up the tree. I laugh out loud.

I want to go over to the monkey and play with him, but I know he will only run away. I sit still and watch him watch me. He darts down from his tree and steals over to a bush directly in front of me. I hear more rustling behind me. I look, and as if my eyes suddenly have adjusted to the woods' camouflage, I see another monkey, and another. Monkeys are all around me, eating, scurrying, and playing.

At this moment I do not bemoan the drought that leaves the monkeys with less to eat and drink. My adrenaline does not flow at the thought of the government's poor planning, given that drought in southern Africa is predictable. Instead, I sit on a rock surrounded by trees and monkey sounds and watch the way the sunlight slips through the shade to reveal the brightness in the land.

# CHINA
(FOUR)

# LEARNING ABOUT SHONA CULTURE

# I  Respecting: Wachikwa

"Mombe" is the word for "cow," I think. I should have paid more attention in Shona class when we learned animal names. I have to admit that "mombe" just didn't seem like a relevant vocabulary word. Now, of course, I find myself facing a whole bunch of animals for which I cannot remember names. After a month in Harare, I am now in Wachikwa, a rural village where I will stay with a family for a short time and learn about rural life. After Wachikwa, I will return to my homestay with the Mandazas.

I follow Amai Kyandere down the dirt path, my skirt catching on the prickly brush. Amai Kyandere is short and somewhat heavyset, and she walks with a sure stride. The folds of her light blue dress are draped across her broad shoulders and her muscular arms and back. She wears a white knit hat, yellow plastic sandals, and a pink, white and blue wrap around her waist.

Cows and goats nibble on the yellow grass around us. I hear singing, and as we round a bend I see a group of at least fifty people sitting gathered around something in the center. Amai tells me, "There is a funeral." The people are huddled around an open grave. Before I have a chance to ask who died, I find myself sitting on the soft dirt surrounded by the singing mourners.

There are many women in the group. The brightly patterned Java print material they wrap around themselves as a skirt and their colorful head wraps contrast with my memory of my grandfather's funeral in Boston. There, everyone wore dark colors, and there was no singing. Amai leans over to tell me that the singing keeps the witches away while the grave is not yet sealed. The circle of mourners begins to part, and several women move into a line by the opening in the circle. The first woman kneels, places a pot full of water on her head, and walks on her knees to the edge of the grave. Once there, she removes the pot of water from her head and pours it onto the grave. Amai tells me the water is to seal the grave.

The singing continues as woman after woman carries water to the grave in the same manner. As the line grows shorter, the women look at me. "Come," they beckon. I walk to the opening in the circle and kneel down. Someone hands me the pot of water, which I support on my head with my hands. I walk on my knees to the grave and pour the water into the open ground. The singing intensifies, then fades as the last woman seals the grave. As people stand up, Amai leads me away from the funeral.

When I woke up this morning in Harare and packed my bag to come to Wachikwa for the "rural stay," I had no idea what I would find. The bus ride on the dirt roads was hot, crowded, and noisy. I was so physically uncomfortable wedged into that bus that I could not think about anything else. There was nothing I could do to become comfortable, so I escaped by falling asleep.

When I exited the bus, being freed was such a relief that at first I didn't even look around to see where I was. When I did, a deep breath flowed through me as I faced the almost silent village in the midst of nothing but yellow fields and green-brown brush. The headmistress of Kyandere School and members of the women's club introduced themselves and took me and the other two women from my program to the headmistress's house for tea.

After we finished our tea, Amai Kyandere told me she would be my homestay "Amai." She then led me outside and started walking toward this funeral. I didn't know where she was taking me as I followed her. She had a quiet, calm manner and I felt comfortable just walking down the path behind her.

In fact, I feel comfortable simply being here. Even though I have only just arrived and am already faced with strange customs, I feel peaceful inside. I feel that I am in the right place and that I am with good people.

I hear laughter coming from the hut, and I follow Amai Kyandere to the doorway. As we kick the dust off our shoes, I look in and see that the eight women from the women's club are laughing at two friends from my program. I start laughing too, at the fluffy, white chicken they are trying to control in their arms. My friend Kelley says, "Perrin, this is our chicken! The women's club gave it to you, me, and Melissa!" They gave us a *chicken*? My mind is spinning through images of us carrying a live chicken on the crowded, ninety-minute bus ride back to the city. What on earth are we going to do with it?

The three of us pose with our chicken, and the women take pictures for us with our cameras. Then I discover the women's plan for the little fowl. Amai Chavunduka pulls out an axe, takes the chicken by the neck and carries it outside. In a moment, she returns with our beheaded gift, puts it on the floor, and invites us to help pluck its feathers. After she cleans it out, she places it in a pot on the fire in front of us. All the while the women are dancing and teaching us the songs they sing while they work. After what seems like a very short time, the once squirming chicken is ready to be eaten. I feel only mildly guilty for thinking it tastes good.

Soon Amai Kyandere tells me it is time to leave. We walk outside and start toward her home, where I will stay. My eyes follow the dirt path through fields of dry yellow grass dotted with brown brush, out to the grey mountains. I've never seen so much space before. As we walk, we pass grazing cattle and goats. After a month of dodging cars, buses, and people in Harare, Wachikwa feels like paradise. The smell of animals and earth are far sweeter than exhaust fumes.

This village has no electricity or running water. To me, everything seems calm without the glaring artificial lights, beeping microwaves, or ringing telephones that I associate with "normal life" in the U.S. Harare lacks many of the "conveniences" of the west, but it has cars, electricity and a city pace. This is a different world. This is "normal life" in most of Zimbabwe.

I don't need to remind myself, however, that within this calm environment, the women are busy. There are none of the conveniences that Harare does have, such as refrigerators, plumbing, or good light after sunset. Appliances common in the west, like dishwashers, washing machines, and vacuum cleaners are unheard of. Women do at least 85 percent of the labor, and the work is strenuous. They also take care of the children, and there are no "day-care centers" or televisions to occupy the young. Though life here is as busy and hard as it can be in the west, it feels less hectic, perhaps because it is not driven by machines. Everything has to move at a human pace.

Amai begins to apologize for the poor condition of her home before we arrive there. With a bowed head and a halting voice, she also tells me that she and her husband have been married for a long time, but "Baba Kyandere and I have no children." In Zimbabwe, children are essential marks of status for a couple.

"That's okay," I assure her.

She replies softly, "No, I wish that I would have children."

"Well, I am sure your home is beautiful even without children."

As we approach her home, I see that my words are appropriate. Only one of the three structures on the property is a typical round hut with a thatched roof; the other two are newer, square structures. As we enter the low gate that keeps goats out and chickens in, Amai shows me two rectangles of land bordered by neatly arranged stones that contain the dried remains of the plants she grew before the drought. It is the first rural home I have seen with nonvegetable gardens. She and Baba also maintain a vegetable garden, though they can water only half of the space because of the drought. I see that they have their own well, but Amai informs me that the water level has dropped too low for them to take water from it; they now use a community well a few minutes away. Amai and Baba dug their well themselves.

Amai shows me in to the smaller of the two square structures. It is the room in which I will sleep, and I am amazed that it contains a bed. I had not expected a room of my own, much less a bed to sleep on. If Amai had children, I might be sleeping on the floor with several others. Once I put my backpack down, the room is not big enough for two people, so we enter the other square structure, that consists of a small sitting room and her bedroom.

In the cramped space are a coffee table, two chairs, and a bookcase, neatly arranged and all adorned with intricately crocheted doilies and hangings. When I admire them, her face lights up, and she tells me that she makes them. I praise her skill, and she beams. Like the doilies, everything about her home speaks of constant attention and care.

That night, as Amai prepares a dinner of sadza and muriwo over a fire in the kitchen hut, she returns to the topic of their infertility and says it saddens her deeply not to have children. "People laugh at us," she tells me.

"Why?"

"Because we are not able to have children."

"They should not laugh at you. You are good people and you have a beautiful home. They should understand that it's not your fault that you don't have children. They should be kind to you."

"Yes, I think so too. I work hard to have a good life."

"There must be medical reasons why you have not had children; have you seen a doctor?"

With a sad face, she responds, "A doctor would cost us about $1,000."

Baba Kyandere does not have steady work, and I am told that a typical monthly income in Zimbabwe is about $300, with typical monthly expenses significantly exceeding that. One thousand dollars in Zimbabwe is equivalent to U.S. $200, but to the Kyanderes, it might as well be a million. Amai tells me that she went to a traditional healer for help, but when she did not become pregnant, she decided that a medical doctor was necessary.

A tall, thin man wearing tan shorts and a tan shirt walks into the kitchen hut. This is Baba Kyandere. He has closely cropped hair, an oval face with a high forehead and a light moustache and beard. I introduce myself, and he begins the evening greeting with a wide, welcoming smile on his face. In the dim light, his teeth shine white against his dark skin. He sits down in a chair and asks us about our afternoon. I feel fortunate that both Amai and Baba speak English well enough for us to have an easy conversation. As we talk, Baba's calm, comfortable manner sets me at ease and I relax back against the wall.

Dinner is ready and our attention shifts to the food. Baba stretches his legs out from his seat against the wall, Amai tends to the pots over the fire and I sit beside her. I watch as Amai kneels to place Baba's food on the low table she has dragged over to him. He thanks her and she resumes her seat beside me on the bamboo mat by the fire. She hands me my food and they watch me closely as I begin to eat, then smile approvingly as I take bites of sadza with my right hand.

Baba asks me if I "know sadza" from the United States. Both Amai and Baba are incredulous when I say that we don't eat sadza in the U.S. They then ask what we eat, how we grow it, how we cook it. I find these questions hard to answer. When I explain that my parents do not actually grow the food we eat, that we buy everything in an enormous, indoor market that is open all day and night, they nod their heads and listen intently. I feel like an alien as I hear my words enter the hut.

As we eat and talk, the sun sets and the room grows dark. The only light is the dying fire and one lantern. Baba and Amai are insatiably curious about me and continue with their questions about my life in the United States. Sometimes they counter my responses with an example of life in "our Shona culture." Amai serves tea heavily sweetened with the sugar I brought for them as a gift. Sugar is a luxury here. Baba takes a sip of tea, then leans forward in his chair, resting his elbows on his thighs. He looks at me and asks,

"What would happen if a Zimbabwean man went to the U.S.A. and asked a woman there to marry him?"

In Zimbabwe, if a man wants to marry a woman, the man gives money to her family as an acknowledgment of her worth in the family. I tell him that men do not do that in the United States and that a family there probably would not accept the Zimbabwean man's gift of money. I decide against delving into issues of western feminism in favor of letting their particular curiosities carry the conversation. He shifts to the more general concept of gift-giving.

"In our Shona culture, if one person offers another person a gift, that person has to accept it! It is not right to refuse it."

"In the United States, if someone refuses to take a gift, that person is saying that the gift is too nice and they do not deserve something so nice."

"Oh." He and I both sit back and ponder what we have just learned.

I add, "But many times when someone refuses a gift, the gift-giver is expected to keep offering it until the other person accepts it."

"Oh." All three of us are quiet for a moment and then we laugh at how strange customs sound when they are explained.

Baba then returns to the discussion of marriage. "You are a young child in this family. In Zimbabwe, you are a child until you are married."

"In the United States I am not a child, because there a person is an adult when they turn eighteen years old, even if they are not married."

"Why are you an adult when you are not married?"

"Well, once a person in the U.S. is eighteen, the law does not treat them like a child. They can vote in elections and they can be sent to jail if they commit a crime. If my culture did not think that even an unmarried person can make adult decisions, I could not have come here." Both Amai and Baba nod their heads.

Amai changes the subject: "Does your Amai in the U.S.A. plow?"

"No."

"No?! Who plows?!"

"We don't have land to plow. It is the same as people in Harare who don't have farm land like you do."

"Does your Amai carry water from the well?"

I shake my head, "No, we don't have wells!"

Baba exclaims, "You don't have wells?!"

Amai asks, "Where does your water come from?"

Stumped for a moment, I then remember the reservoir near my house in the U.S. "There are large places, like lakes, full of water that is cleaned and then sent through pipes into houses."

I don't know if my explanation makes sense, but Amai is already asking a new question: "Does your Amai in the U.S.A. cook?"

Should I try to explain home-delivered food, microwave ovens, frozen dinners and take-out? It's getting late, I am tired, and it is true that my "Amai in the U.S.A." is the one who puts food on our table, so I simply answer, "Yes." Amai and Baba nod and smile; I feel as if I have finally given them an answer they can relate to. I can now go to bed feeling slightly less like an alien from outer space.

It takes me a while to find things in my backpack by candlelight. I would like to write in my journal or even do some reading, but instead I decide to go to sleep. Something about the gentle pace of my day makes the effort of locating the journal or book seem unnecessary and contrary to the mood. This village is having a calming effect on me. I relax on my bed, leaving the blanket Amai provided for me folded in the corner. It is far too hot for a cover.

As I lie there, I see Amai walk by my open window and shut it from the outside. She has told me to close it to keep "thieves" out, but it is hot, and I cannot imagine any thieves finding this village, not to mention the fact that the window is so small no person could fit through it. Then I recall my language instructor in Harare having mentioned that many Shona people believe evil spirits come out at night. He said that sometimes people refer to the spirits as "thieves," maybe so that others will take them seriously. I certainly don't want evil spirits coming in my window, so I leave it closed.

Even through the closed window, I hear drumming in the distance. According to Baba, the drummer is practicing for a funeral ritual that will take place Friday night through Sunday. It is a haunting sound, this steady drumming that presses into the silence. Its slow rhythms nudge me into sleep.

After a peaceful night, I am awakened by Amai at 5:30 in the morning. I walk outside and see the clear sky and dry land glowing in the peach sunrise. The crescent moon is about to set behind the mountains. Amai has warmed a bucket of water for me over the fire so that I can bathe. I appreciate her thoughtfulness and effort, and I feel bad that she has used firewood simply so I can bathe. I tell her that I know it takes time to cut firewood and that I don't mind bathing with cold water. From the matter-of-fact way she pushes me and the bucket of water out of the kitchen, I gather that my protests have failed and that I will have warm water every morning.

After a breakfast of sadza porridge and an egg, Amai and I leave to collect water from the well. Six other women, also filling their buckets, greet Amai and me cheerfully with the morning greeting, "Mangwanani!" I look around and wonder why no children have accompanied the women to the well. Children are a central part of Shona communities, and because the Kyanderes have none, I may not experience that aspect of family life. For Amai and Baba, that lack must feel tremendous.

I try to carry one of the large tin buckets on my head as my Amai does, but I seem to lack the talent, and all the women laugh. They laugh harder when I tell these muscular women that the large buckets are so heavy that it's hard enough for me to carry them with my hands. It takes about fifteen minutes for each of our four trips to the well. If I were not there, Amai might have made eight trips to provide enough water for just one day of cooking, drinking, cleaning, bathing and watering the vegetables.

Once we have retrieved enough water, we wash the yellow aluminum dishes and pots using dirt as an abrasive. Then we water the garden. While she takes care of the chickens, I scrub the kitchen floor on my hands and knees and polish it, using some cow dung wrapped in rags. Something in the cow dung makes the floor shine. Before I left for Zimbabwe, someone told me I would gain a new perspective on what is "clean" and "dirty." Cleaning in this way is important work to keep a nice house. We do not have mops and vacuum cleaners here to keep our hands and faces away from the floor; even the brooms we use are only two feet long and require us to bend down.

I consider my friends in the United States and wonder what they would think of this kind of work. I try to imagine what I would have thought of it before coming here, but I realize that I cannot actually remember how I thought before. This place and this moment are the only things that seem real to me. I carefully clean every inch of the floor until Amai looks in and says I've done a good job and now can wait for her until it is time to go to the Women's Club.

The women in the village formed the club for company and assistance while doing their work. They cook and sew together and even help each other build houses. Children often come along with their mothers. Everyone in the group seems to enjoy singing and dancing, and they often make up songs about the task they are working on. The women also spend a lot of time teasing one another and laughing. Amai seems to work faster when the time nears for the club to meet. She doesn't like to miss the gathering.

Amai never asks for help, but when I offer my assistance she usually accepts. This time, though, she tells me that I should study. Instead of studying, I lie down on my bed. My window is open, but the air in the room is stiflingly hot and musty. Still it is nice to have privacy for a moment. The blue wool blanket underneath me prickles my skin as I settle my body against the lumpy mattress. I begin to think about the fact that since I arrived in this village, I have been doing "women's work." Terms such as "slaving over a hot stove" have taken on a new meaning. Even though I cooked and cleaned in the U.S., I never felt that my being female required that I perform those tasks. In fact, I probably would have labeled such a requirement "sexist" and refused to participate. I have been calling myself a "feminist" for a few years, though I have not felt greatly affected by sexism. Of course, I have experienced such eye-openers as the male professor who never calls on me or the other females in class and grades me lower than he does my male classmates. Still, I have always insisted that I am too aware or too strong to be oppressed by sexism.

Now, however, I learn that these issues are much more complicated than I had considered. I find myself in a remote village in Zimbabwe where it is clear that because I am female, I will help with "women's work." While at one time I might have thought that my reaction to a gender-based division of labor would be automatic, now I feel only curious and ambivalent. The women I work with all seem exceptionally strong and aware. They do not have bland, subservient natures, but are just as spirited and colorful as "liberated" women I know in the U.S. I ask myself what it means for these women to have a seemingly subordinate role in their communities.

I have always assumed that "women's work" must consist of the most demeaning tasks. It is true that women do menial, time-consuming work here, but it is also true that both men and women recognize how important and demanding those tasks are. I have not yet heard anyone in this village belittle the work that women do. Still, even if a man is unemployed and has nothing to do, he does not help his overworked wife with certain tasks. My Baba knows how to make tea, and they both chop firewood and plow, but he does not cook or clean. It occurs to me that although it appears that men are the central force in this community, in reality it is the women who run almost everything. If the women did not accept an inferior status, it seems to me that the only basis on which the men could claim superiority would be their physical strength.

The men do not do anything that looks more important than women's work. The economy is very poor here, and men all over the country are out of work. Normally the men would be farming. People in this village used to be able to live off their farmland and sell the surplus. Because the drought has ruined their farms, they have no surplus to sell, yet they need money to buy the food that they used to be able to grow. The drought has also taken away farming jobs, as well as jobs in the city, that men used to hold.

Baba jumps at the chance to work, even if it is just to help someone for a day. Frequently his employers fail to pay him. Not knowing if there are any laws that could help him collect his wages, he feels powerless to claim his wages. Baba and other men in the village spend a lot of time doing nothing or looking for jobs that do not exist. Many are dejected and humiliated. The women, on the other hand, are as busy as before. I wonder if it doesn't make the men feel even worse to see their wives busy while they don't contribute their share.

My Amai derives a great deal of pride and satisfaction from doing her work well and keeping an orderly home. She stays up late crocheting because she can try to sell her doilies, but also because it is something she is good at and enjoys. She likes to make pretty things. She does not seem to feel demeaned by doing "women's work." I also have not felt demeaned by it, partly because I am trying to learn about the culture and to do that, I must understand the role of women. Additionally, I know that I can be proud of this work and its value, and feel that those around me respect what I do.

Yet when I am not actually participating in the work it is hard to avoid the fact that no matter how much pride the women take in their work, or how important it may be, they cannot choose whether they want to do it or not. Men in Zimbabwe don't have many choices either. Especially with such a depressed economy, men all over the country are limited. But when I think of the male musicians I know in Harare, it seems to me that men do have more choices than women have.

In truth, I have little insight into the male experience in Zimbabwe. Being female, I am expected to spend my time with other females. What I know of the men comes from a few, specific relationships, such as with Baba Kyandere, the musicians in Harare, or from listening to Amai discuss the issues. Aside from these sources, I can only recall the signs in Harare declaring there are no jobs available or walk past the groups of men idling on the sidewalk all day long. However, I spend a lot of time with women, and their sex dictates that they take responsibility for most of the labor required to maintain a home in the village, while the men remain unoccupied.

When I carry out a task, I focus on the task itself or on its context in daily life here. But as I lie in bed and think of my Amai toiling away from five o'clock in the morning until half-past eleven at night, it makes me sad that she has little choice. I don't know how she feels about her long work day. She is sad about the drought, Baba not having work, and their inability to have children. She certainly may wish that she did not have so much to do. In fact she has told me that she feels she is too busy. On the other hand, that does not mean that she would be willing to have her whole identity in the community turned upside down.

It is hard for me to form a cohesive set of opinions on this matter because my thoughts come from two completely different realms: my experience with people in a Zimbabwean village and the feminist opinions I have brought with me from the U.S. Gradually I resolve to remain present in my experience and simply do what feels right. I trust myself in that respect, and this resolution is the only answer that makes sense to me. My feminist perspective from the U.S. may shape what I notice here or how I understand what I notice. However, as someone who is learning what it means to have true respect for a way of life that is completely different from the one I know, I feel no need to value my old perspective more highly than the one I am discovering here. I prefer to let each one find its place inside me, and it excites me to imagine the richness of what I am gathering.

The women from the club are meeting in Amai Chavunduka's kitchen hut, which is large enough to hold all of us. We sit on the floor, drink tea, and chatter. Predictably, someone begins to sing. My Amai and her sister-in-law stand up to dance. Amai always dances. This time she picks up her eight-month-old nephew. As she sings and dances and holds this child, I am mesmerized. There is an intensity in the way she holds the baby, and I feel her joy and longing through voice and movement. I don't know if I am imagining her emotion, but I cannot shift my gaze to see if anyone else notices her. She is not looking at the baby; she is not looking at anything. Her eyes are closed or staring at the space just above the floor. Her voice carries over all the others. I hear the song nearing its end, and I don't want it to stop. Desperation flows through me suddenly as I realize she is going to stop dancing, sit down, and probably return the baby to his mother's arms. As the singing fades into talking, I look at Amai, who is now seated, quiet and still, her arms empty. She looks at the same spot in the air. I can only wonder what she sees.

The candlelight casts an orange glow in a circle on my paper. Two mosquitoes buzz near the flame. I am writing in my journal and can only slightly see the words on the page. I like not being able to see what I've written. It keeps me from getting caught on an idea once I've written it down. All I can do is follow my thoughts, even if they flow crookedly off the lines, or don't particularly flow at all.

Once again, Baba, Amai, and I had an interesting conversation at dinner. They tried to teach me new Shona words and idioms. Both Baba and Amai refer to me by my Shona name, "Tonderai," or call me "mwana," which means "child." They seem proud when they call me "mwana." I love the way they say "Tonderai" because their accent is beautiful to my ears. My Shona name means "remember." Hannah picked it out one evening in Harare when she was helping me learn vocabulary. Although Hannah already had a Shona name, I gave her another one: "Imbai," which means "sing." Often I caught her singing when I walked into our room.

During dinner, Baba informed me that tomorrow we won't speak English anymore. I told him that in that case, our conversations will be much shorter tomorrow than they have been. He laughed, though I really wasn't joking. Before I had a chance to panic over the thought of having to communicate solely in Shona, he sprang another rule on me: When I see him in the mornings, I am to kneel and greet him. I also am to kneel when I give him something, such as food, as well as when I want to ask a question of him. When he finished his "request," both he and Amai looked at me. I don't know what they expected me to say, nor do I know what I wanted to say, but I felt uncomfortable with this new rule. I said I would do it but that in the United States women and children don't kneel for men, and I am not accustomed to it. They nodded their heads. Baba told me that in their culture, kneeling shows respect. I understand that; I just don't know if it's how I want to go about showing my respect.

My back begins to stiffen from crouching on my bed next to the candle, so I close my journal and lie down. As an afterthought, I blow out the candle. Candles are not abundant here, and I have already gone through one in just a few nights. The smoke twists through the air, filling the darkness with its waxy odor. Without the candle to distract them, the mosquitoes migrate toward me. I swat them away, then close my eyes to picture myself kneeling for Baba in the morning. My immediate reaction is that I cannot possibly kneel for a man. It goes against everything I believe about how the world should be.

I take a deep breath and try the thought again. Does it really go against everything I believe? Or am I actually ignoring what I believe about respect, culture and relationships simply because of preconceptions I have brought with me from the West? Baba and Amai respect me. I can tell that by the questions they ask and by how intent they are on teaching me about their culture and themselves. They listen carefully to what I say about my culture and try to understand my point of view. They have worked hard to incorporate me into their lives, to make me a part of their small family.

What would happen if I refused to kneel? What would that communicate to Baba and Amai? I worry that it might communicate far more than my stance on sexism. It might communicate my personal disrespect for Baba and Amai. Moreover, my position here is different from that of a Zimbabwean woman, who might choose to make a statement by not kneeling. Not only am I a guest, but one from a different culture. I came here asking them to share their lives and their culture with me. Of course, I am by no means obligated to do everything they ask. But the idea of rejecting a custom that they tell me is about showing respect does not coincide with my personal feelings toward them and the relationship we have been developing.

In some ways, what it means for a Zimbabwean woman to kneel for a man is different from what it would mean for me. Sometimes I feel that being a white person from the U.S. places me just outside the circle of meaning that customs here hold. Even when I participate in the customs, I do not lose my identity as an outsider from a part of the world that exerts power over this part of the world.

The more I participate, however, the more I demonstrate my respect and acceptance of the value of a culture and a people. In many ways, the people here are constantly told that they are not valued in the world. As a representative of a part of the world that frequently contributes to that message, I want to express a different sentiment.

As I let these thoughts settle, I begin to realize that their asking me to kneel may actually be an invitation, an honor. They are allowing me to be a part of their culture. I now have the chance to show my respect for them and for their culture on their terms, in a way they will understand and appreciate without needing any interpretation. The act of kneeling for Baba would also be a challenge for me to let go of my culture for a moment. Freeing myself for that moment might allow me to touch a part of another culture.

The broader principle I see behind having women kneel for men deeply disturbs me. On the other hand, I feel that the value of my presence here is less about principles than about human beings. Once again, I find myself believing in two incompatible perspectives. I remind myself to be present in the moment. I can lead my life according to principles, but only if they match what feels true and right within me and within the context of my relationships.

I sit up and stretch, and then walk outside. The moon has not yet risen above the mountains, and there are more stars than I have ever seen. The night sounds here are subtle, and that sometimes fools me into thinking that everything is silent. But if I pay attention, I hear all the unique sounds of nature that chime together until they become one song. I breathe deeply and the clean, earthy air fills me. As an almost imperceptible breeze floats over me, I feel like smiling. I return to my room and fall asleep instantly.

After bathing with the warm water Amai prepared for me, I head toward the kitchen hut for breakfast. I see Baba step out of his room to take care of his cows. Part of me feels like pretending I didn't see him. I stop myself and turn to face him. He watches as I slowly pick up my skirt and lower myself until my knee rests on the yellow dirt. I begin to clap my hands together in the formal manner and initiate the morning greeting. He claps his hands together too and starts his response to the greeting.

I watch his face and feel as if my mind and body are separate in this moment. My mind studies his serious expression and my kneeling form. I see my body communicating to Baba that I respect him and his culture, and I see it thanking him for respecting and welcoming me. As we complete the greeting, I know that my mind and body actually are not separate; in fact, they are completely joined in conveying a single sentiment. We finish, and I stand up. A smile spreads across his face.

Baba follows me into the kitchen and proceeds to talk quickly to me in Shona. When I remind him that I cannot understand him very well, he pauses for a moment. "I'm sorry, I forgot," he says. He smiles at me again and heads out the door. Amai gives me twice as much porridge as usual and begins to tell me our plans for the day.

# II  Participating: Kyandere School

I sit on the wooden chair with my feet flat on the floor and my hands clasped on my lap. Amai Moyana and I ignore the flies buzzing around us as she serves tea. Amai Moyana is the headmistress of Kyandere Primary School, where I have volunteered to teach English while I stay in the village. She is a petite woman and better dressed than anyone I have seen in the village. She wears a mauve and white flowered dress and white earrings. I think she is the only person I have seen here wearing jewelry.

I feel I should look "professional" for our meeting. Unfortunately, my T-shirt is stretched out from too much hand-washing and line-drying, and my skirt is torn from the time in Harare when the wind blew and my skirt attached itself to the fender of a parked car. Amai Moyana's dress doesn't look brand new either, but she has an air of professionalism. Her posture is perfectly straight, and she holds her head high.

As a rule, Zimbabwean women have excellent posture from learning to carry things on their head when they are young. Amai also looks everyone straight in the eye and has a friendly but firm manner of speaking. At this meeting, she will tell me about her school and we will discuss my placement as a teacher. She hands me a cup of tea, and I thank her in my most formal Shona manner. She looks me straight in the eye and responds in a very business-like way, "No sweat."

Amai begins to describe the school. There are 601 students and 15 teachers. Eight teachers are female, seven are male. Amai Moyana came to work at Kyandere School as a second grade head teacher. Her first project was to put a roof on the Block 1 building. She matter-of-factly informs me, "It came off in a storm." As headmistress she has several goals, including creating a "powerful and more advanced, better water supply," having "the recommended ample and modernized restrooms," and building a bell tower and an attractive sign post.

Amai has made changes in the school since becoming headmistress. For instance, one classroom had been vacant for years because in 1984 a child was struck by lightning in it, so people didn't want to use it. Amai made them use it. The preschool used to be held under a tree because there were no available rooms. The thought of trying to teach and contain a class of six-year-olds under a tree makes me shudder. Amai Moyana had a haunted house renovated for use, rationalizing that it is haunted only at night. Now it serves as a six-room preschool. There are three preschool teachers for children six years old and under. Unfortunately, they do not always come to work because they are paid so little.

With help from their "twin school" in Norway, Amai has developed the Culture Hut to "counteract" the influence of western culture on the students. Earlier in the morning, she showed me the hut. Painted red triangular patterns decorate its outside walls. Inside the small structure are old Shona musical instruments, clay pots, clothing and written explanations of each object.

As I was looking at the beautiful objects, I thought about the infinite ways in which western culture has intruded on the precolonial societies. Kyandere Primary School may have a "Culture Hut," but the school is modeled after the British educational system, and classes and exams are in English. Does the use of the British school setting to educate children about precolonial life imply submission to the same culture Amai strives to "counteract"? Or does it show a society flexible enough to adapt to new systems while still maintaining a sense of its cultural history and the value of that history?

I tell Amai Moyana again how beautiful I found the hut and its contents. She proceeds to tell me that her school offers intramural sports, a percussion band, and a competitive traditional dance group. I notice the coexistence of western sports and "band," with Shona percussion instruments and traditional dance.

In Zimbabwean schools, fundraising does not include the bake sales that my schools always relied upon. Instead, students collect empty cooking-oil bottles and resell them. They also help sell chickens and produce from the school garden. Although parents must pay for their children to participate in extra-curricular activities, Kyandere Primary School is fortunate to receive financial support through a Norwegian "twin school" program. In 1991, the school was able to build its library with program money, and parents in the community contributed four bookcases. The Norwegian assistance this year, Zim $27,307 (approx. U.S. $5,460), has helped the school upgrade its garden and water systems, renovate and equip the library, and purchase administrative supplies and sports equipment. Amai Moyana points to her meticulous, handwritten accounts in a large book with thick, beige paper. I wonder what the school would be like without the Norwegian money.

Amai explains that with free public education, enrollment is high, which creates a strain because the schools cannot absorb all the students. As a result, if students fail the important Grade Seven exams, they are not encouraged to try again. If they do choose to try again, they can seek permission from the Secretary of Education. I want to ask what the future may be like for students who don't pass the exams, as well as for those who do. I also want to know whether anyone ever tries to obtain permission to re-take the exams. However, Amai continues her rapid, enthusiastic exposition, and my questions fade as I wait for her to pause.

The Grade Seven exams subjects are Shona, English, math, content (religious and moral studies), social studies and the environment, with two hours devoted to each subject. To encourage competition among teachers, the school displays the number of passes and failures in each teacher's class. Amai remarks that many students fail the exams because of difficulty with the language, since the exams are in English, or because of problems at home that affect the student's ability to prepare.

Amai Moyana keeps a close eye on the attendance registers. This year attendance has been low because of the drought and the Economic Structural Adjustment Program affecting parents. Many parents may not be able to afford building fees, for example. There are dropouts in all grade levels and among both sexes. After eight consecutive absences, the student's teacher will talk to the student's parents.

Poor attendance is not always the parents' fault. Amai Moyana recounts that one boy gave the lack of school books as an excuse for having missed weeks of school. However, both of his parents work and his teacher says he does have books. His punishment is to write out his falsehood one hundred times. As I listen to Amai, a male teacher enters to complain that although he has "persisted" in trying to obtain exercise books, many of his students have no materials.

After he leaves, Amai volunteers information that it never would have occurred to me to ask about: She says that although corporal punishment is not allowed in the classroom, certain behaviors warrant "strokes" by the headmistress or deputy headmaster with a witness present. While I was growing up, corporal punishment at school (against state law in California) was not something I feared. According to Amai, the behaviors that may result in "strokes" include smoking, gambling and having love affairs, among other offenses. I ask how she might know about a "love affair" between students, and she replies that love letters and inappropriate drawings would tip her off.

We finish our tea and the flies settle on our empty mugs.

Another teacher comes in, a young woman, who invites me to observe in her classroom. Amai Moyana says, "Yes! Tomorrow you go with Amai Ndanga!" I thank Amai for the informative discussion, and again she assures me, "No sweat."

The next morning, my Amai wakes me earlier than is normal so that I can be ready for school. As it turns out, I have enough time to bathe, eat breakfast, help collect water from the well, and dry some dishes before I go. As Amai has no watch, she repeatedly asks me for the time. When she determines that it is "time to go," she begins to walk me toward the gate. At the gate, I pause to say goodbye to her, but then I realize that she is going to walk me all the way to school. We live less than two hundred yards from school, so I am surprised that she is going to accompany me.

She takes my arm and walks purposefully up the path to Amai Moyana's office. In the office, she and Amai Moyana chat a little, but mainly she tries to be quiet as the headmistress gives me directions to my classroom. Only after I make it clear that I know where I am going does Amai leave. The classroom I will be in is only four doors down from the office, and I arrive there without getting lost.

I sit in the back of the room and watch as the students tumble in with bright, excited eyes. They see me and giggle, then file into their seats, pushing into one another in their hurry. Once seated, they stand again and all together say, "Mangwanani, Mistress," to their teacher. She responds, "Mangwanani, students. You may sit down." They sit and return to their chatter. She comes over to me and gives me some books to look over and explains what the lesson will be this morning. Then she returns to the front of the room to begin class.

As their teacher stands before them and asks a question, I notice that most of the forty-two little heads turn to the back of the classroom. I stare back at them. Why are they looking at *me* when their teacher has just asked them a question? She repeats her question, and when I persist in doing nothing, the children gradually turn back to her. She asks the question again, and this time it is as if an electric current has zipped through the room. Suddenly arms wave frantically in the air; children almost fall out of their seats vying for her attention. Some students blurt out their answers, unable to keep the knowledge from spilling off their tongues. I almost laugh, but I don't want to draw their attention again.

There was no need for my concern; within minutes half the class has resumed staring at me while the teacher begins her instruction. Thinking I should set an example, I try to keep my eyes focused on the teacher. Unfortunately, I am as curious about the students as they are about me, and I have to fight to keep from looking back at them. When I accidentally catch a student's eyes, I smile and she collapses into giggles.

I try hard to appear engrossed in the lesson. After a short time, I actually find it interesting. I seem to have forgotten a lot of what I learned in the second grade. Today I am only observing, but tomorrow I will teach my own English and Math lessons. The teacher tells me I will teach my lessons right after her section on "religious and moral teachings." All the lessons are taught in English, except for religious and moral teachings, which is taught in Shona.

I open the books Amai Ndanga left me. The illustrations show more black than white children. Both Shona and European names are used in roughly equal numbers, although in reality more Zimbabweans are Shona than European. As I look over the use of pictures of black children and Shona names in lesson examples, I wonder what books are used in the elite white schools.

This classroom does not look drastically different from my own second grade; there are long green chalkboards, alphabet cards with sample (English) words, and mobiles hanging low from the ceiling with vocabulary words on them. On the walls are pictures of animals and trees. However, one section of the pictures is labeled "God's Creations." In my public school, animal pictures might have been in a section on "Science" or "Evolution." All the pictures are faded and the mobiles tattered. I remember my second-grade classroom as colorful, with changing displays throughout the year, and I had my own work space. In this room, there are only four tables, with anywhere from four to six bodies crammed on each wooden bench. Two of the tables have twelve children at them and two have nine. They are grouped according to ability: slowest learners at one, fastest learners at another, and merely slow and merely fast at the other two.

Lunchtime arrives quickly, and I go home and eat sadza with my Amai. Baba has already eaten and isn't home. After we eat and wash the dishes, it is time for me to return to school to observe a remedial English class. Currently, there are fifteen students in a remedial math class and twelve in the English class. Amai Moyana says that two teachers are "partially trained" for remedial classes. Exams are given regularly to these students, and many pass.

In the one-hour class I am observing, only half of the twelve students are present, mostly ten- or eleven-year-olds. When the teacher asks questions, the children hesitate, hide their faces, avert their eyes, and remain silent. Their behavior contrasts with the enthusiasm of the second-grade class I observed earlier in the day. I wish I knew what different experiences have led these students to be in the remedial class, and what different thoughts run through their minds as they sit here.

The teacher shows me a log of the students' progress. There are columns for identifying the students' "specific problem" and the teacher's "objective," "methods," and "evaluation." The columns fall under headings of comprehension, reading comprehension, prepositions, and tenses. Some of the teacher's evaluation comments include, "can do better if she stops being lazy," "should learn to work on her own," "it's only that she was not careful," "he should read single words; paragraphs are just too much," "confidence is what she lacks," and "is very active and full of determination." These fragments of description make me want to get to know each student and learn what a broader description might include.

The log has a page listing the students' health, their parents' occupations, and the names of those with whom they live. I am surprised to see that only two of twelve live with both their parents. Others live with grandparents, aunts, or only their mother. It is likely that many of the absent parents work or are looking for work in the city. Under the column "parents' occupation," one occupation per family is listed, but does not specify whether it is the mother's or father's job. Some occupations listed are tobacco-curer, tire-fitter, peasant, builder, mechanic, soldier, cook, yarn-weaver and electrician. Three are peasants. Many of these jobs may be in the city.

Amai Moyana sits with me and, at the fifteen-minute break, gives the teacher feedback. She remarks on individual students and suggests specific lessons that may help them. Then she compliments the teacher on her patient and encouraging teaching manner. When Amai invites me to comment, I offer that small-group work might motivate shy students to participate and encourage more people to think without waiting for the teacher's answer. Even though I've never taught before, both Amai Moyana and the teacher welcome my opinion.

At 7:10 a.m. on Wednesday, the entire student body assembles outside. They line up by classes, which results in rows of blue-uniformed children rising taller and taller. Once they are in line, their teachers inspect their appearance. The poverty in the village makes enforcing standards of appearance nearly impossible. Although virtually all the uniforms have been handed down many times over and are dirty, ripped, and/or in the wrong size, the teachers accept them, knowing the students have no choice. The students' shirts must be tucked in and collars folded down, but they don't have to wear shoes because they may not have any. Even their fingernails are checked for dirt, but no child is turned away for having dirt under her or his nails. After the inspection, everyone sings the African national anthem in Shona and returns to class.

I resume my post at the desk in the back of the classroom and observe the Grade Two math lesson. The students are involved in a counting game. Amai gives a bunch of bottle caps to each table and tells the students to divide the caps equally. She comes over to me and tells me I may walk around and check on the students' progress. Glad for the opportunity to become involved, I approach each table quietly so that I don't distract the students. I find that when I act like a teacher, they do not feel as compelled to watch me. I also find that the spirit of competition has conquered mathematical reason: at each table, one or two students triumphantly display their possession of the majority of bottle caps.

After the counting game, Amai writes math problems on the chalkboard, and students volunteer to answer them. They are practically bursting from the benches trying to be called on to go to the board. Even students who do not seem to know how to answer the problems want the chance to write the numbers on the board.

During the written part of the math lesson, Amai explains that some students cannot do their work because their parents cannot afford paper. Amai laments that she used to provide paper for them, "but not these days," with the economy so poor and inflation high. I look around and see a large number of students sitting idly while their classmates scribble out equations. I rip pages from my journal and give them to the students. The children without paper have already been sitting for ten minutes while the others work out problems. One student, eager to begin her work now that she has paper, breaks her pencil lead. Amai hands her a razor blade to sharpen her pencil.

Even though I give them enough paper for today, they won't have enough for tomorrow. I glance at my journal and see all the pages full of my thoughts and observations. How lucky I am to be able to write as much as I want. I tear out more paper and leave it on Amai Ndanga's desk for the next few days. It still won't be enough for the next day, and I don't know what to do with that thought.

I imagine myself as one of these students in a faded, handed-down uniform, crowded onto a bench with too many other restless bodies. In front of me, there is a small space at the table for my arms to squeeze into, but because I have no paper to write on, I try to keep my hands still in my lap. I will be sitting here for a few more hours. Some other students around me do have paper; some do not. It is hard for those of us without paper to sit still because we have nothing to focus on. Maybe I poke the student next to me who has paper, interrupting her work. Maybe the teacher admonishes me for being disruptive. I am bored, and I wonder why I am in school.

Who would I be now if I had attended a school like this when I was growing up? Would I have been motivated to go to college? Perhaps I would have dropped out of school long ago. The curious and interested minds in this room have a challenge ahead of them much greater than any challenge I faced in school.

After math, Amai gives the students a break by having them sing a song. The boys stand and sing in Shona about "Amai cooking sadza" while the girls sit on the floor singing and acting out cooking sadza. They all sing at the top of their lungs. What a twist it would be if the boys were the ones acting out the cooking.

Singing is followed by a Social Studies lesson about "Work and Leisure," including a picture identification exercise. In the picture, a woman is holding a broom. The children observe, "mother is sweeping." Amai Ndanga confirms, "Yes, she is a mother, and she is sweeping." As far as I can see, however, there is nothing in the picture that indicates whether she is a mother or not. The picture shows only a woman sweeping.

It occurs to me that gender-socialization is much more striking in a foreign culture. Since in one's own culture, socialized roles and behaviors appear "normal," it may be harder to see when gender rules are being conveyed. Here where little seems "normal" to me, the gender role-playing leaps out at me.

Next the children list five tasks around the house: cooking, washing, sweeping, pounding grain and plowing. They are to determine who performs each task. The correct answer is "Amai" to every one of the tasks, though the students add that children can sweep and plow. No one mentions Baba. The teacher concludes the lesson saying that children should help their mothers. As an afterthought, she points out that fathers may plow, and boys may help their fathers.

Amai then begins the art lesson by drawing a pattern on the board for the students to copy. She gives the fastest-learner table her master copy of the pattern for guidance. It seems to me that the slower learners might benefit more from that copy. I wonder if students deemed "slow learners" are automatically considered slow in all areas. I wonder if anyone checks.

I peer over the students' heads to look at their work. Supplies are low. There are two black crayons and two red ones for four tables. They are broken in half so that all four tables have one of each. However, there are nine to twelve students at each table. The pattern calls for three colors, so the plain paper must stand for one of the colors. I want to reach into my memory and pull out my Super Box of Crayolas with 100 colors in it and give it to the children.

The next morning, I arrive at 7:00 a.m. to find the students present but not the teacher. A boy is drawing on the chalkboard with three different colors of chalk. He draws a woman wearing a head wrap, sweeping a yard with chickens in it. Behind her is a hut and a woman pounding grain next to it. There is also a field with a woman plowing. This boy has created a strong image of women as workers. I think of second graders in the United States drawing pictures of cartoon characters.

The other students chatter and play word games but become restless after about fifteen minutes. I have no idea what to do, but it seems that I should assume some sort of control. I walk to the front of the room. I actually could stay in the back because most of them are watching me already.

In the same tone of voice I might use if I were telling someone she's just won a hundred dollars, I tell the class we can sing a song. I start teaching them "Old MacDonald Had a Farm," but the truth is I don't know how to teach. At first I ask them to repeat after me, but when I realize that is too difficult, I write each line on the board and point to it. That works much better and they do an excellent job. It is hard for me to focus on teaching them the song because their enthusiastic, earnest cooperation and bright, respectful faces absorb me to the point that I want only to watch their expressions. Once they have learned the words, I ask each of the four groups to come to the front one at a time and sing it with me alone. Then we all stand and sing it together. At that moment, with perfect timing, Amai Ndanga arrives. Sitting at our seats, we sing it for her in unison, and she claps in appreciation. Then she begins to teach them fractions. I am glad she arrived when she did.

The fraction lesson is entertaining. Amai asks the class, "What is half of six?" A few students call out, "Three!" She asks again, "What is half of six?" Several more yell, "Three!" Again, "What is half of six?" The whole class has caught on: "Three!" She asks them, "What is half of *three*?" They yell, "Three!" Math is so hard!

Physical education lasts about ten minutes. The students play "Ring Around the Rosie" and then run to the bathrooms. Afterward it is time for the music lesson. Amai hands out instruments to the students. The fastest-learner table of eleven children and the fast-learner table of twelve receive nine instruments at each table. The slow-learner table of eleven receives only two instruments. At the slowest-learner table of ten children, there are four instruments. It seems to me that with twenty-four instruments and forty-four students, a teacher could figure out a more equitable way of dividing the instruments.

I go over to the slowest-learner table and ask them about their instruments. I don't want them to feel unimportant just because they were given fewer instruments. After I spend time with students at both the slow learner tables, I notice that they do just as well as the faster learners. Maybe some of them would not be such "slow learners" if they were given more attention.

For the last lesson of the day, I teach spelling. After my warm-up this morning with "Old MacDonald Had a Farm," I feel like a tenured professor. I successfully manage not to betray my own confusion while teaching the British spelling of "plough." As I look out at their serious, shy, eager faces, I feel like thanking the students for taking me seriously even though I am just a student here myself.

After school, I am included in a faculty meeting. Amai Moyana arrives late, and as she takes her seat she declares, "So, leaders are never late. They are always *delayed*." The meeting begins with a prayer. Amai opens a discussion of the upcoming "Open Day" for donors to come to see where their money is going and where it is still needed.

The first issue is "will all the visitors be fed?" Amai responds they should try to feed everyone, "even parents and the children." This means feeding nearly the entire village. One teacher counters that there is not enough time to raise money for food. Another asserts that each of the fifteen teachers should give $10 (approx U.S. $2) from her/his own pocket. One man proposes to take money from the building fund. The woman across from me thinks that only important people should be fed. Amai Moyana is firm that "everyone if anyone" should be fed.

Amai tells us she is in the process of printing a letter asking for donations from members of various committees. One teacher begins speaking in Shona, but Amai stops him and reminds him that for my benefit they must speak in English. He switches to English and asks if the donation plan will work considering only two weeks are left until the event. Amai responds, "It will work even if we have to break our arms and legs to make it work." I believe her, but the Grade Five teacher becomes upset and asks if that means they will have to "give up the teaching of children." Mr. Matiswa, the deputy headmaster, responds that they will hold the Open Day no matter what, so the negative attitude must go. He then gives a short, inspirational speech about their duty as teachers, and everyone relaxes. Afterward when Amai Moyana asks for my opinion, I offer some suggestions for time-efficiency based on fundraising I have done in the United States.

As the faculty meeting comes to an end and the teachers begin to thank me for coming to their school, I realize that tomorrow is my last day at Kyandere Primary. I feel involved in the school now, and it seems strange that I will not help plan the Open Day or be there for it. While teaching may not be my professional calling, I feel a part of Amai Ndanga's Grade Two class, and it seems that the students and I are just becoming used to each other. Each morning I look forward to their excited, curious smiles. Each day I feel disturbed by the lack of supplies and how this lack affects the students. As we break up the meeting, Amai Moyana reminds me to come early for the assembly tomorrow.

I look out at the 601 students standing in perfect order in their old uniforms, and at the group of teachers standing off to the side. In the bright morning sun, all the colors before me look washed out. Yet I feel the energy of the young group as friends stand next to each other and only half listen to the announcements. Amai Moyana comes to the microphone to give a formal speech, thanking me for my contribution to the school. Afterward she approaches me again to express her appreciation. I can think of no other response but "No sweat." She gives me a wide smile and a firm hug, then we face the flag and join in the singing of the national anthem.

# III Belonging: Wachikwa II

It is 5:30 p.m. and the sun and sky begin to fade into dusk. At this moment, I am a part of the landscape I see. Nine women walk along a dirt road that cuts through an expanse of wild fields stretching to the foot of the distant mountains. There are no sounds but the varied rhythm of bare or sandaled feet striking the earth. The group spreads across the width of the road. One woman has a baby held to her back by a blue and green wrap. All the women wear long skirts, and some wear headwraps. They walk at a relaxed pace; they are not in a hurry. Softly they laugh and joke and chatter. Someone begins to hum. The hum becomes louder as others pick up the tune. Words are added, and the humming becomes singing. The women begin to dance as they move down the road, dancing and clapping to the rhythm of their song. The sun sinks behind the mountains, sending shimmering gold beams through the clouds. The women continue singing and dancing along the road until they reach the village. As they return to their separate homes and duties, their humming does not fade. Long after the darkness has enveloped the last rays of sunset, the rhythm beats softly in my mind.

Because I have been busy with school, I have not seen much of the members of the women's club. My Amai's sister-in-law, also called Amai Kyandere, has come to see me this morning with her eight-month-old son held to her back by a faded red and brown wrap. As usual, we sit on the floor of the kitchen hut. She pulls her baby onto her lap, and my Amai builds a fire so we can have tea.

My Amai's sister-in-law loves to tease people, and she tells me that my boyfriend has missed me while I've been at school. "What boyfriend?" I ask. Laughing, she insists that my boyfriend has told her he missed me *terribly*. Again I ask, "What boyfriend?!" She exclaims, "Him," and points to her son. I look down at the tiny body. His huge, gleaming brown eyes dance from one of us to the other, and his smile is the most joyful I've ever seen. He clutches my long hair with one of his strong, miniature hands. "He's my boyfriend?"

"Yes, I'm giving him to you!"

"Thank you!" I guess that's the appropriate response.

"You can hold him."

She drops him into my lap, and his energetic body squirms into my arms. He is still smiling at us, and I cannot imagine a sweeter boyfriend than this. If only he'd let go of my hair.

I can hardly believe tomorrow is my last day in Wachikwa. In one way, I feel as if I've been here forever. Everything is so comfortable now. Amai, Baba, and I have our routine down perfectly. I bathe first, then Baba bathes while Amai prepares breakfast and I prepare for school. After breakfast, Amai and I collect water and Baba leaves for some unknown place. I think he usually goes to a friend's house, but he says that before the drought and when the economy was better, he would go to work either on his farm or on someone else's. Then Amai and I wash the dishes, and I leave for school. Between school and dinner, Amai and I either join the other women at the women's club for a short time or chop firewood. Afterward, we prepare dinner, and Baba joins us. Every night, the three of us talk for a long time after dinner. After they go to bed, I write in my journal or sit outside for a while. I enjoy every minute.

It amazes me how much I have seen and learned here. Sometimes I imagine myself as an infant just beginning to understand the world around me. I know there is so much in this village that I have looked at without seeing. I would love to stay in Wachikwa longer and learn how to see, feel myself grow. I know I will come back to visit Amai and Baba, and it is OK that I have to leave because I leave with a new reality. A window opens where there once was a wall. Words appear where before there was only a blank page. This new reality has shown me a different view and has given me the words to form questions that may lead me to a larger understanding.

For the first time, I am awake before Amai. The mosquitoes buzz near my head, and it is dark outside. I open my door quietly and step outside onto the soft, cool dirt. There is nowhere for me to go and nothing for me to do, so I sit down on the ground. Amai and Baba will think I am crazy if they wake up and find me here, but the morning chill and the quiet solitude feel so good that I can't move. I watch the waxing crescent moon sink and the first pink rays of the sunrise spread out from the horizon. The roosters begin to announce the morning, and I know that Amai will be up momentarily. I stand up and walk toward my room so that I don't scare her. She walks outside just as I reach my door.

"Tonderai!" She is surprised to see me.

"Mangwanani, Amai. Marara here?" I begin the morning greeting: Morning, Amai. Did you sleep?

"Ndarara kana warara wo." I slept if you slept.

"Ndarara." I slept.

"Tatenda, Tonderai." Thank you, Tonderai.

In a mixture of English and Shona I point out, "I am awake before you this morning!"

"Yes! Are you OK?" She looks concerned.

"I'm fine! Nothing's wrong, I just woke up."

"Oh, OK." She looks at me for a moment and then says,"Tonderai, I have something for you."

"What, Amai?"

"A gift."

"Why do you have a gift for me?"

"Stay here. I will come right back." She goes back into her room.

She has a gift for me? It has been a gift to have stayed here and been a part of her life. She returns with a plastic bag in her hands and places it in mine. I open it and see a crocheted doily. She has made this for me. I touch it lightly and feel the circular, cream-colored patterns. It is beautiful. I look up at her.

She tells me, "I begin making this for you the first night you are here and I work on it every night. Tonight is your last night here and you now have it."

I do not know how to express my gratitude. "Tatenda, Amai. This is so beautiful. You must have stayed awake so late to finish it in time. Thank you. I love it."

"Now you remember me in the U.S.A."

"I would remember you anyway. Now I have another reason to remember you. Tatenda chaizvo, Amai. I love it *so much*." I wish I knew how to communicate how much I value this gift.

"Zvakanaka. Now, you help sweep and I will warm your bath water." She turns around and walks toward the kitchen hut.

I pick up the little broom and begin to sweep the yard. She likes it swept so that the pattern in the dirt looks like two rainbows with their ends overlapping. One arm's-length swish curving to the left, one arm's-length swish curving to the right, in rows up and down the yard. I don't know why we sweep the dirt, but the patterns are pretty.

Because it is our last day, the women from the club have baked a cake for me and the other two students from my program. Flour and sugar are luxuries, so the cake is an extravagant gesture. They baked it in the ground. Amai explains to me that they burn wood in a shallow pit, and when the fire dies but the wood is still warm, they put the cake on top of the wood. Then they place a metal cover over the pit and burn cow dung on top of it. They burn the dung for as long as the cake needs to bake. The cake is warm, soft, and moist in my hand. As the first small piece meets my tongue, it fills my whole mouth with delicious sweetness. After a week of eating only sadza and muriwo, I cannot be distracted from this cake from the moment I first hold it in my hand to when the last piece dissolves on my tongue. We each eat one square, and some people even eat two. After we finish it, we sing and dance. The women try to teach us some of their dances and laugh at our attempts to copy them. They want us to teach them some dances, but we don't really know many to teach.

I had asked my Amai if I could buy two more doilies from her for good friends at home, so she has brought some to the club. A couple of the other women show us theirs as well, but none are as beautiful to me as my Amai's. Kelley and Melissa also buy some. Amai asks twenty dollars each for the two I choose, which totals about eight U.S. dollars. It seems so little money for such intricate handmade work, so I give slightly more than what she has asked for, and I hope the money will help them. We continue dancing and singing until the sky begins to darken and it is time for the women to return home and make dinner.

Amai and I walk home slowly. I notice that I have acquired the habit of lifting my feet a little higher off the ground to avoid the prickly weeds that scratch my sandaled feet and ankles. I've also become accustomed to the cows grazing by the path, and I think nothing of pushing one a little to the side to make room. When we reach the house, Amai heads straight for the kitchen as I wire the front gate shut to keep out the goats.

I pause for a moment before following Amai into the kitchen hut. That this will be my last dinner with Amai and Baba feels momentous. I am anxious to pay attention to every detail so that I can remember this night, along with the previous ones, as clearly as possible. I walk inside and take my seat on the bamboo mat beside Amai. I watch as she manipulates the three pots on the fire: one for sadza, one for muriwo, and one for hot water. She is humming, so I ask her to sing for me. She laughs and begins to sing in Shona until she asks me to bring her another spoon. I tell her that I have a tape recorder, and ask if she will sing into it later on. She laughs again and says she will; she's never heard herself on tape before.

As usual, just as the hut begins to darken and Amai lights the lantern, Baba walks in and sits down on his chair next to the narrow door. I lift myself up on my knees and recite the evening greeting to Baba. He responds with a large grin, and then asks me about my day. He enjoys hearing my interpretations of what I have done and seen. When I remark on how the women baked the cake earlier, he asks how women bake cakes in the U.S.A. He laughs when I appear confused about how to answer his question and teases me, "You don't know how to bake a cake!" Thinking of boxed cake mixes, milk in cartons, and electric ovens, I agree, "I guess I really don't know how."

Despite my confession of incompetence, Amai trusts me to help stir the sadza. The wooden spoon is strong and doesn't break as I push and pull it through the sticky, heavy mixture. I continue dragging the spoon back and forth as the sadza thickens and my arms begin to tire. Amai turns to Baba and tells him that they will sing into my tape recorder after dinner. He nods his head and smiles. Finally, the sadza is ready and we can eat. Tonight we do not discuss any major social issues or make grand comparisons between Zimbabwe and the United States. Instead, we chatter about how Baba's cows are doing, whether Amai watered the vegetables, and how preparations for the school's Open Day are progressing. Eventually we look down at our empty plates and realize we are finished with dinner.

Amai begins to gather our plates and the dirty pots for washing in the morning. I remind them about singing for me and run to my room to retrieve the tape recorder. It takes me longer than I'd expected because there are no lights and I can't find the matches to light a candle. Finally, I locate the tape recorder and dash back to the kitchen, worried that Baba might have left. Fortunately, both of them still sit exactly where I left them, patiently waiting for me.

When I sit down, Amai reaches over and takes the tape recorder from my lap. She looks at it from all angles and holds it carefully in both hands. I show her the "record" button and encourage her to press it, but she hands the recorder back to me and tells me to do it. I record us talking for a moment and then play it back for her. Both Amai and Baba laugh when they hear our voices coming from the small black box. I give the recorder to Baba, who examines it closely in front of the lantern and then looks at me questioningly. "Baba, don't ask me how it works! I have no idea!" He laughs, giving the recorder back to me so they can sing. He and Amai tell me, "We will sing a song for your Amai and Baba in the U.S.A." I nod and say, "Tatenda chaizvo. They will love that very much."

I settle back against the hard wall and tuck my skirt around my crossed legs. Amai puts down the teapot and stretches her legs out before her. Baba sits up straight in his wooden chair. They look at each other and then at me. I tell them, "You can start whenever you are ready." After a moment of silence, then Baba takes the recorder from me and announces into it, "Ndini Baba Steven Kyandere. Ndiri kuda imba...na Amai." ("I am Baba Steven Kyandere. I want to sing...with Amai.") I ask Amai if she wants to say something as well, but she declines, laughing. They talk for a moment in Shona, and Amai begins to sing.

Amai's strong voice bursts into the room, and Baba's blends with hers. They are smiling and their eyes are bright. Both lean forward slightly, as if to push their voices into the center of the room. They sing in Shona, and I can't understand any of the words, but it doesn't matter. As they near the end of the song, I inhale the air that feels rich with their voices. They close the moment with a deep, drawn out, "Yahhh-ahhhh, yehhhh."

I play the tape back for them three times and they are proud of their song. They ask, "You will play this for your Amai and Baba ku ['in the'] U.S.A.?" I assure them I will. Finally, Baba yawns and says, "Ndiri kurara." He is going to bed. I wish him a good night, "Marara zvakanaka, Baba." Amai and I stay in the kitchen to finish our tea. She is very quiet, and I wonder what she is thinking about.

She asks me, "Will you send me photos of you, please?"

"Yes, Amai. I promise I will."

"I will send them to my own Amai and tell her 'this is my child,'" her voice softens as she repeats, "This is my child."

I cannot think of how to respond to this honor, so I just nod and look at her in silence.

She continues, "My Amai will be proud that you are my child."

I notice that the light of the fire makes her eyes shine, and then I realize that they are filled with tears.

"Amai, why are you sad?"

She is quiet for a few moments and looks down into her tea cup." I am sad because I cannot have children," she tells me. "It is very bad. I married Baba when I was fifteen and a half years-old. He was twenty-five. It is sixteen years ago. After one year, when I had no child, Baba's parents are very angry. They tell Baba to divorce me or take a second wife. A second wife to give him children. So he marry another wife. But his parents tell the second wife's parents I am cursed. They say I will curse their daughter so she can have no children too. Her parents demand he divorce me or they take their daughter away." Amai wipes the tears from her cheek, and I exhale the breath I had trapped in my lungs.

She continues, "Baba would not divorce me. He says to his parents, 'I have built all these walls with Revesai and I will not divorce her.' He sent the second wife away. His parents still are angry and they hate me. I ruin their son's life. He is supposed to have babies. And all these years he loves me and still I have no baby.

"If it rains this season, maybe we sell enough vegetables to have money for the doctor. I work very hard to have a nice home and to have money for the doctor. I crochet very late, even when I am tired. I don't know how to build babies, but I know how to build other things. The other people laugh at me and Baba for not having children.

"Please send me a photo of you so I can show my Amai my baby in U.S.A. And send me a photo of your Amai ku U.S.A."

"Amai, I will send you those pictures. I know you are sad that you don't have children, and you would be a wonderful mother. You have been wonderful to me while I have been here. But, there are other things for you to be happy about. You have so many reasons to feel proud. You know that you 'build' beautiful things. You have the most beautiful home in the village. Your doilies are better than everyone else's. All of the women in the women's club love singing and dancing with you. And Baba really loves you. He would not have sacrificed his relationship with his family and having children if he did not think you were worth it. He knows he is lucky to have such a good wife. I wish you were not so sad."

"Tonderai, I am happy you came here. I know I work hard and make nice things. I work very hard to have a nice life. But sometimes, it is too sad to not have a baby. Now I have child in the U.S.A., so maybe I am not so sad."

She smiles at me, and though I know that their having a "child" in the United States is not nearly enough, I am glad that the thought provides her with some happiness. I wonder why she and Baba have not had children. All the responsibility seems to lie with Amai; everyone assumes the problem is with her body, not his. It is unlikely that they will ever have enough money to see a doctor, even if the rains do come.

I think of the doily she crocheted for me each night after I first arrived, the water she warms for me each morning, her walking me to school on my first day, her closing my window at night to protect me from "thieves," and how she gives me extra helpings of food at dinner if at any point in the day I mention that I am hungry. As these thoughts travel through my mind, it becomes clear to me how much the desire for a child, someone to care for, is a part of her. The prejudices of her culture and its pressures only compound the lack she already feels. In Shona culture, a female is not considered a woman until she has a baby. I know that nothing I can say or do will improve her situation. All I can give her is my respect and admiration.

"Tonderai, we sleep now. Tomorrow you leave, and I want you to have sleep."

"It is fine if I am tired tomorrow. Do you want to talk more? I don't want you to go to sleep feeling like you are bad because you don't have babies."

"I hope it is right what you say. I hope it is right that I make other good things."

"Amai, you know you make other good things. It still is sad that you have no children, but you should be proud of yourself for other things."

"I hope so, Tonderai. Now, please, we will sleep. Don't forget to close your window."

"I know, Amai."

"There are thieves."

"I know, Amai. Good night."

"Warara zvakanaka, Tonderai. Ndichakuona mangwana." Sleep well, Tonderai. I will see you tomorrow.

She leads me to my room and waits as I lock the door and shut my window, then calls through the closed door, "Ndafara kuti Tonderai anorara mu Wachikwa." She is happy because I sleep in Wachikwa.

The women from the club tell Kelley, Melissa, and me to be at the roadside to wait for the bus out of Wachikwa by ten o'clock in the morning. They don't mention that the bus does not adhere to a particular schedule and that we may wait for it for hours. More than ten women from the club wait with us. I release my backpack onto the dry, dusty roadside and feel sweat trickle down my back. I squint in the bright, hot sun, and see my Amai watching me. When I smile at her, she begins singing. The other women pick up the song, and soon we are all singing and dancing. Caught up in the songs and the playful, teasing way the women include us, I forget that I am about to leave the village. I feel more a part of it than ever.

Because the roads are dirt and there are no cars, we can hear the bus and see the dust fly up from the road long before it reaches us. After many songs and a lot of joking, we hear the first rumble of the old engine and see the cloud of brown dust billow behind the crest of the hill. We predict how much more time we have before it arrives, and suddenly we are all quiet. I look from one face to the next, and see smiles and tears.

Someone touches my arm, and I turn to see my Amai looking at me with eyes full of tears. "Amai, tatenda. Ndichakutonderai." Thank you, Amai. I will remember you. "Tatenda, Tonderai." Thank you, Tonderai. She gives me a firm, short hug, and then looks up to see the bus careening down the bumpy road. We both say at the same time, "Tichaonanazve!" We will see each other again. We laugh, and she squeezes my arm. It is time to go.

I step onto the bus and find my way through the awkward bundles of vegetables and baskets of chickens to a small space where I can stand. The bus driver has tossed my backpack on top of the bus, and as we buck and jerk down the road, I have no confidence that I will ever see it again. I turn to look out the window and have to stand on my toes to see over the head of the boy beside me. I look out at the group of women singing. I see my Amai with a smile on her face as she sings and watches the bus roll away. I will see her again.

# IV  Reacting: Phone Call Home

Maybe I was wrong to write to my friend in California about having knelt for Baba Kyandere. When I spoke with my parents, they said my friend had called to tell them about it without providing any of the context I had so deliberately included in my letter. My parents were shocked that I actually had knelt for a man. When they commented on it, I had such an urge to hang up the phone and disconnect myself from their perceptions, my perceptions, the complexity. I felt helpless to explain what really had occurred in that village, especially in an expensive long-distance call with a poor connection. I felt incapable of explaining that I had not lost my self-respect, been oppressed by a man, and succumbed to blatant sexism in a primitive culture.

The village of Wachikwa is where I grounded my sense of what it means to respect another culture, another people, and another way of life. In this village I could kneel before Baba and feel valued by him rather than degraded. Yet I know that nothing could make me kneel for any man in the United States or for others in Zimbabwe. This place is where I began to think about what "respect" means and how people show it.

Baba would not divorce Amai even though it meant sacrificing his relationship with his own family and his status in the community, in a culture in which family and community are valued above anything. His action was one of love and respect for Amai and for their relationship. When Amai kneels for Baba, she shows him the respect she feels for him. He shows his respect for her each day in the way he speaks to her and treats her. The act of a woman kneeling for a man may be a symbol of the inequality of the sexes. However, for Amai and Baba Kyandere, the act is about respect.

Women should not be valued less than men in any culture for any reason, yet it is clear that women are subordinate in Zimbabwe, as everywhere else. I cannot imagine a man kneeling for a woman here. I am critical of the sexism in this society. I don't like the fact that women kneel for men and that men never kneel for women. However, it is important not to be blinded by preconceptions or fixated on judgments. Along with being skeptical or critical, I have learned that I must listen and respect.

I do not know how to describe the integrity, intelligence, and sensitivity of these people. If their behavior appears backward to an observer, then that observer may have to look more closely. The Kyanderes are adhering to the norm of their culture, just as people elsewhere try to do in their own cultures. The Kyanderes are adhering to their culture with a sense of pride and dignity; their actions are not about giving or taking power, but about respect.

If Westerners think poorly of the position of women in African cultures, then western governments and business should not perpetuate subordination of women by dealing solely with African men. It is far too rare that western donor organizations ask African women what they need to improve their lives, rather than talk only to men about "development." For example, when a man requests money for additional farmland from a western donor, he may not mention that his wife will be responsible for much of the additional work that the land will require. There are ways to address the issue of sexism in Africa far more constructively than simply by passing judgment. Moreover, if people address sexism in real ways on every level, the sexist dimensions of practices like kneeling may change or fade away.

The fact is I had expected to feel degraded when I knelt for Baba. I was surprised when I actually felt elevated in his eyes for having performed that simple act. Since that time, only people in the West have threatened to degrade my experience with Baba. Because of my own expectations before kneeling for Baba, I do understand the astonishment of my friend and my parents at learning that I had knelt for him. Perhaps the hardest part of being here is communicating with people who are not.

# SHANU
(FIVE)

# UNDERSTANDING WOMEN IN ZIMBABWE

# I  Awakening: Issues Facing Women

The newspaper article is only five lines long, but it grabs my attention. Practically hidden in the middle of Zimbabwe's Herald is an article that says a woman was sentenced to eight years in jail for "dumping" her three-month-old baby. Other than offering a brief reference to the woman's having suffered from a "depression," the article gives no information about the circumstances of the case. I have never heard of "baby dumping," and I wish the article were longer. I cannot help but wonder what it would be like if women, instead of the government, controlled the news media. I finish reading the article as Hannah sits down with her breakfast of fried eggs bathed in tomato and onion sauce, and a cup of milky tea.

"Hannah! In this article, it says a woman 'dumped her baby.' What does that mean?"

"In Zimbabwe, women do that when they don't want their baby."

"Does this happen often?"

"I don't know, but I've heard stories." Hannah did not look half as concerned by the issue as I felt.

"Why do women do this? Can't they give the baby up for adoption?"

"I don't know! People do not have adoption very much, I think."

As I reflect on the article, the topic of my Independent Study Project becomes clear to me. For almost a month, I have been looking for a topic but have been unable to decide on one. I want to study an area that feels important to me and that could contribute something to Zimbabwe.

During the last month of the program, we are to complete projects on the topic of our choice. When we finish them, we will give copies to any organization in the country that may benefit from them, or to the University of Zimbabwe library. The reason we will give our projects to institutions in Zimbabwe is so that we don't gather information merely to take it out of the country, but we also give some back. With the subject of "baby dumping," I suddenly have a topic that inspires me.

"Hannah, can you imagine how that woman must have felt when she decided to dump her baby?"

"No. I think she would be very sad."

"What do you think leads women here to decide that they need to dump their babies?"

"I don't know. I would not do that."

"What would you do if you had a baby you did not want?"

"I would go to my sister's house."

"What if your sister had no money and could not take you in?"

"I don't know. I would have no place to go."

"So what would you do?"

"I don't know. I would need money to feed the baby."

"Could you get a job?"

"It is hard to get a job with this ESAP [Economic Structural Adjustment Program]! I hope I could make money! But I will not have a baby I do not want. I know this."

When I awoke this morning, I did not know that I was about to embark on a quest. Now I am on my way to the Zimbabwe Women's Resource Centre and Network (ZWRCN) to see if they have any information on baby dumping. Questions spin through my mind: What is the status of abortion rights here? What are the economic prospects for a single mother? What are Zimbabwean society's expectations of women regarding sex, birth control, motherhood, education and employment? How do those expectations coincide or conflict with one another? What assistance is available to women with unwanted pregnancies or to their unwanted babies? Beyond wanting to know why baby dumping occurs, I am looking for reassurance that there are forces working to prevent it. I want to find out that women who have unwanted pregnancies have reason to feel hope and have places to turn to for help.

ZWRCN is practically hidden, and I walk past it a couple of times. It is on the second floor of a nondescript building in a relatively unpopulated section of Harare. No identifying sign is visible from the street. I wonder why the "Resource Centre and Network" does not have a visible sign so that people know it exists and can have access to it.

I open the door and am greeted by a woman eating lunch at a desk who tells me she is the secretary. She adds that nobody else is there, but pointing next door tells me I can look around if I'd like. I walk into a small room lined with bookshelves and with an island of tables set up in the center. This must be the "Resource Centre." I put down my backpack and look at the shelves of books. Each section is clearly labeled: "Maintenance Law," "Marriage," and so on. Above each label are articles, books, reports and pamphlets on the subject. Although there is not a section on baby dumping, I am sure I will find other useful information here.

On a separate book rack, I see that ZWRCN has a collection of feminist literature from different countries. There is Gloria Steinem's recent book, Susan Faludi's *Backlash*, books in French, books from Britain, and books from other African nations. For a moment, I revel at the sight of a collection of feminist thought in the corner of a room in a nondescript building in Zimbabwe. The women who wrote these books did so because something was important enough to them to write about and that they believed could also be important to others. This small collection with all the different books it holds, proves the truth in the authors' ideas and in their belief that those ideas could be important to others. Discussion of feminist thought takes many forms and affects people all over the world in different ways. I am filled with a sense of hope and strength from evidence that in spite of obstacles, women are reaching each other and giving and gaining new perspectives on being women in this world.

Sometimes I have experiences here that give me hope, yet I am constantly aware of a reality that can feel like a mass of granite, grey, hard and dense. I arrive home before dinner and take a few moments to review my notes on ZWRCN and check my homework assignments. Hannah walks into the room as I examine the books I borrowed from my program director's house: *Independence Is Not Only for One Sex* and *Mothers of the Revolution*. The title of the first book refers to the idea that when Zimbabwe became an independent nation, Zimbabwean men were liberated but the women were not. The second book is about the women who were a part of the liberation struggle. Hannah tells me she has read parts of that book because the previous student who stayed at the Mandazas house had also checked it out, and Hannah borrowed it from her. She had never heard of it before Judy brought it home.

As I review my Shona homework after dinner, Hannah picks up *Independence Is Not Only for One Sex*. I comment that I agree with the title, that I think independence should not be for one sex only. She nods her head emphatically and in a firm tone says, "I think so, too." I ask her if most of the women she knows agree with her that women should not have to do all the cooking and cleaning and should have the same opportunity as men to do other things. She says, "Yes." Then I ask what the men think of that idea. She says, "They are lazy." They would not do housework. After that remark, she avoids any further discussion of the matter. It feels as if the limits she is aware of in her life have extended to what we are able to talk about.

As the time nears when we usually go to bed, I notice that she is still reading the book. When I glance up and see her eyes intently focused, both hope and sadness wash over me. Hannah's mind is open to new perspectives, and the brightness in her eyes reveals her excitement at what she reads, at the thought of a new way of living. But her body is still, and she is silent. All the ideas remain caged within her. There is nowhere, given her current situation, for them to go.

I cling to signs that eventually Hannah will find a place outside her mind for her ideas. She has told me that if she ever has sons, she will teach them to cook and clean so that they may help regularly with housework. She believes that if she and her boyfriend get married, he will "allow" her to raise her sons in such a way. Sometimes even the words she chooses gnaw at my sense of hope.

I do not see the *Independence* book again until a couple of days later, when I come home from school. I find it lying on my bed in the exact spot where it was when Hannah first picked it up. She hasn't mentioned anything, but I know she has read the entire book. Just as she puts the book back in its place, so she continues to live within the constraints and expectations the book decries. Yet I know she believes in what she has read and that she will always be looking for an opportunity to live differently. The strength that moves her through each day of a life she does not believe in is the same strength that may eventually move her into a place where she may live true to herself. Crossing the time and space between the two points will be long and hard. A Zimbabwean writer said, "Colonialism created another hunger and drought. To me that was the spiritual hunger and drought." The same could be said of any kind of oppression.

As I look through my notebook, I uncover some literature I took from ZWRCN. According to the pamphlet, the organization has been open for only two years, since 1990, ten years after Zimbabwe gained independence. Perhaps places like ZWRCN can be potent new forces in yet another struggle for independence. It is clear to me that independence for one sex only is not independence.

Shona class ends and after rushing to ZWRCN to return a book, I meet some friends for a movie. I had invited Hannah to join us, but she had seen the movie last year. The Zimbabwean film called *Neria* is about a woman who lives in the city with her husband, Paul. They both work, and their marriage is based largely on a sense of respect and equality. When Paul is killed in an accident, Neria suddenly is mired in a conflict between "tradition" and "modernity" over inheritance laws.

Shona Customary law is a system based on Shona cultural traditions and followed by many Shona people, but it is not considered valid under Civil law, which is the British-derived system upon which Zimbabwe's government is based. According to Shona Customary law, Paul's family has the right to, and responsibility for, his bank accounts, property, children, and wife. Historically, the system ensured that everyone in a community would be provided for. A woman would not be abandoned after the death of her husband; she might marry one of his brothers, who could care for her (polygamy was practiced in the event that the brothers were already married). As social circumstances have been changing, the law is not necessarily appropriate and has been abused.

In the case of Neria, for example, the bank accounts that Paul's family claims because Paul is now dead, were actually joint accounts that include Neria's own earnings. In addition, Neria does not want to marry Paul's brother or have her children live with him in the rural village. She wants to continue living in the city with her children and to manage her own affairs. Unfortunately, Paul's brother is greedy and uses the Customary Inheritance law to acquire all of Paul's material possessions and money. But Neria learns that according to the Civil Inheritance law, she has the right to maintain possession of Paul's property and their money, as well as to retain custody of their children. Neria takes the case to Civil court and wins.

Throughout the movie, the conflict between tradition and modernity is shown to be serious but not insoluble. Paul's mother is at first strongly opposed to altering tradition in any way. She lives in the rural village and disapproves of Neria's "modern" way of life. She believes Customary law is right.

However, as she slowly becomes aware of how Paul's brother, her surviving son, is "misusing tradition" to fulfill his greedy desires, her mind opens to Neria's perspective. By the end of the movie, she supports Neria's court victory because "tradition says family must be cared for and it will be," with Neria having custody of her children. Finally she tells Neria: "You have shown me that at times we have to bend our traditions to the changing times. You are a strong woman."

I think about the dynamic nature of every culture's traditions.

They evolve according to the needs, resources, and interests of people within the culture. At one time it was traditional in the United States to hunt a turkey for Thanksgiving dinner. Now most people buy their turkeys. It used to be traditional in the United States for men to work outside the home for and women to work inside the home. Now two-income households are the norm. In Zimbabwe, too, traditions are evolving.

Once something is labeled a "tradition," however, it seems to take on a special sanctity. Many people in the U.S. seem to look back at the 1950s with nostalgia, thinking of a smiling mom in an apron baking apple pie, despite the fact that many of those moms were not happy or satisfied with their position in life. Traditions in Zimbabwe also tend to be idealized, even when the reality of their impact is not necessarily positive.

It seems that in every culture, different groups of people use the word "tradition" to fight for or against change. However, traditions mean different things to different people and may be interpreted in many ways. I appreciate how the elder woman in *Neria* accepts the need to adapt the traditional inheritance practice in order to fulfill its original purpose, which is partially to ensure that the family of the deceased is provided for.

Occasionally during the movie, I find myself thinking of my baby-dumping project and the social pressures on women. *Neria* shows how strong the idea of "tradition" can be and how it can affect women's lives. The rigid view of a tradition that a man uses to give himself more power and wealth leaves Neria trapped and powerless until her friend tells her about the Civil Inheritance law. I wonder if other cultural beliefs and practices make women feel trapped and powerless and influence the occurrence of baby dumping. I also wonder what cultural beliefs and practices might support women, leading them away from dumping a baby and toward finding a positive solution.

At other points in the movie, I think of Hannah and women like her who have seen the widely viewed film. A popular Zimbabwean musician portrays a brother of Paul's who supports Neria in her fight. The message of the film is one of respect, fairness, and flexibility. After spending time at ZWRCN and seeing *Neria*, I am once again full of thoughts about

Zimbabwe's difficult present and images of a future based on respect, fairness, and flexibility.

When I arrive home, Hannah is cooking dinner. I clear some dirty plates off the counter and begin helping her cut tomatoes, onions, and greens. I tell her that I saw the movie and that I really liked it. "Yes, I liked it, too," she says. It has been a long time since she saw the movie, but as I talk about it she remembers it clearly. While I cut the vegetables and she stirs the sadza, she begins to sing the movie's theme song, "Neria." Her voice is soft and light as she carries the mood of the movie into our kitchen.

When dinner is ready, the boys take their plates into the living room. Hannah and I drag chairs through the kitchen to the back yard. Only the light from the kitchen illuminates our space as we eat in the cool evening air. Every so often, Hannah begins to hum the song, and I sit back and listen. It is nice to take something beautiful from a memory, lesson or thought and then sing it into an evening over dinner in the back yard.

As I walk up the stairs to ZWRCN, I notice a sign on a second-floor door that says, "Women in Law and Development in Africa/WiLDAF." Thinking that this organization might somehow be relevant to my project, I wander in. A woman at the door tells me that everyone is at a meeting, hands me some literature on the organization, and points to a chair.

I look over the information and read WiLDAF's "statement on organization," which outlines the founding of the organization and its objectives. According to the statement, "WiLDAF is a regional network dedicated to promoting and strengthening action-strategies that link law and development to empower women and improve their status." The network includes fourteen African nations. The stated objectives are clear and action oriented, and its list of priorities appears well thought out. The first item on the August/September calendar is fundraising. Requests for money are being made to several U.S. corporations, foundations, and organizations.

I have never heard of WiLDAF or of organizations like it in

daily conversation with Zimbabweans, and I am surprised that it exists. I imagine that most of the general public does not know of organizations like WiLDAF and ZWRCN. WiLDAF was founded in 1990, the same year as ZWRCN. Maybe two years is not enough time for such progressive organizations to settle into the consciousness of mainstream Zimbabwe. Yet their presence, their energy and their incipient movement to empower and improve the situation of women indicate the potential for positive change to come.

I make it into the kitchen after fending off an overly eager Naranga, who wants to play. Hannah is in the kitchen washing dishes, even though she normally prepares dinner at this hour. Sometimes her schedule is thrown off because of electricity rationing caused by the drought. Usually it is turned off for a few hours in the morning or evening, several nights a week. I don't like it when the lights are out in the evening because the streetlights go out, making it unsafe to walk around outside. We cannot make dinner, and I cannot do homework. Shutting off electricity in the city also means water-purification plants do not have power. We may need to start boiling our drinking water if rationing continues.

However, this evening the lights are on, so I ask Hannah why she is not cooking dinner yet and where the dirty dishes came from. She tells me that the boys used all the dishes in the kitchen to make themselves food while they watched TV. I can hardly believe they actually cooked for themselves. Apparently Hannah was out buying food for the family. I ask Hannah if they offered her any food when she returned, since she always cooks for them. She says they did not offer her food, but they left all the dirty dishes for her and it's taking her a long time to clean them.

At that moment, the boys enter the kitchen and say something in Shona to Hannah. They look agitated, and Hannah does not respond to their remarks. After they leave, Hannah tells me they were complaining that she did not yet have dinner ready. They said they were hungry, and she should cook dinner immediately. However, she cannot cook dinner until she has washed the pots they dirtied, because she needs them to cook with. I ask Hannah why she did not suggest to them that if they had cleaned up a little bit, she could have started making dinner sooner. She says that she tried suggesting that a long time ago, and they threatened to hurt her physically if she ever said anything like that again. "So I am silent," she says.

I take a deep breath and walk across the kitchen toward the living room. But I turn around. What could I do or say if I went into the living room and confronted the boys? What could I do or say that would actually help Hannah?

"Hannah, do you really think they would hurt you?"

"Yes."

"Can you tell Mr. Mandaza and Amai?" Although Hannah isn't their daughter, they have taken her into their home, she is a blood relation, and they seem to genuinely like her.

"No. They will tell the boys and make them very angry."

Hannah and I do not speak for a while. I cannot think of anything to say. I cannot believe anyone would want to hurt her. I cannot believe that those boys get away with such behavior. I finally understand why Hannah locks the door to our bedroom and hides the key where the boys will never find it: in the bag of clothes-pins in the kitchen. Until now I could not picture Kenneth and Marcus being malicious. Maybe this is also why Mr. Mandaza locks the phone so that no one can use it without his permission.

One part of me wants to help Hannah with the dishes to make her evening easier, and another part wants to let the dishwashing take a long time so that the boys are forced to wait for their food. I decide to help Hannah because upsetting the boys may hurt her in the end. When they return to the kitchen to get the food Hannah finally is able to prepare, I am disgusted. I walk outside instead of conversing with them, and wait until they have retreated to the television before I return to the kitchen. I don't know how Hannah can stand living like this. The hardest part for me is accepting the fact that she has no choice.

I have always felt that violence and oppression are unacceptable and that it is unacceptable to compromise on those issues. Now I find myself forced to accept the unacceptable. I see no alternative; she and I both have to accept the injustice she lives with. This concept eats away at me and at my most deeply held beliefs about right and wrong.

I ask her how we can change her condition, and she tells me we cannot. She is an intelligent and resourceful person, but this time I hope she is wrong. I am certain there are systems affecting her that need to be and can be changed and that there are people working to improve lives like hers. But I also know that no change is going to take place fast enough to ease my mind or remove her from this injustice.

As the bus jostles me back and forth against the people I am standing between, I try to remember what I want to ask the director of the Zimbabwe National Family Planning Center. I am headed there now because I am eager to get started on the research for my project. It is not yet the official "Independent Study Project Period," but I am excited about my topic. I am interested in interning at Family Planning for a couple weeks in order to gain some sense of the everyday family planning issues of women in Harare.

I leave the bus and look around for the building. Just as I see a group of women I can ask for directions, a man walks up to me and asks under his breath, "Do you want to buy some pills?" Although I do not know what kind of pills he has in mind, I am sure I do not want them. I shake my head and walk toward the women. The women congregating for a class are friendly. They point to another building to show me where the director's office is located. A man is mopping the wooden floor of the building when I enter. He asks who I am looking for, then tells me the director will arrive shortly. As I wait, I write a letter for the director in case she does not arrive by the time I need to go home. After about fifteen minutes, a man walks up to me and tells me to follow him. He seats me in a chair in a tidy but plain office and takes the seat opposite me. He does not introduced himself, but suddenly it occurs to me that he may be the director. I had thoughtlessly assumed that the director of Family Planning would be a woman.

I explain who I am and that I am interested in volunteering here.

"Why you did not send me a letter of introduction first?" His question surprises me.

"I am sorry. I am not familiar with the process of obtaining a volunteer position in this country. As I said, I am a student from the United States. I only have a few weeks to study family planning and I did not think to write a letter first. I hope that this meeting can serve as an introduction."

"Normally, I see a letter of introduction."

"I am sorry. Maybe this letter will help." I hand him the letter I wrote while I was waiting for him, along with a copy of a more official letter of introduction our director gave us for this sort of situation.

He skims the letters and looks back at me coldly. I tell him again why I am here and emphasize that I am willing to act in any capacity that will be helpful. He tells me he will call me soon and let me know if I may volunteer. As I leave, I have a disappointing feeling that I will not hear from him. I was not prepared for such a difficult meeting and negative response.

I am learning that official Zimbabwe is a far more formal place than the United States. I am also surprised by the cool reception he gave me. Almost everyone else I have met here has been accommodating. Was my behavior, though polite, not formal enough? Or is my being female, white, young, foreign or all of the above a factor?

I am also surprised that he is not open to having me volunteer. In the U.S., most organizations seem to welcome volunteer workers. I feel willing to help and participate. My wish to contribute is as strong as my desire to learn here. It surprises me that my volunteer time is not wanted.

Maybe he thinks I am intruding. He is the first person I have met in Zimbabwe who has responded negatively to me. I am curious to know what it is about me, him, and the situation that inspired his reaction. Perhaps Baba Mandaza will have an answer for me. As I squeeze myself into a small space in an E.T. heading in my direction, the sky is fades into sunset and I look forward to dinner.

When I arrive at the house, Baba Mandaza greets me, and I sit down with him in the living room. I tell him about my disappointing meeting with the head of Zimbabwe National Family Planning. When I try to explain why I was disappointed and ask him why the man was cool toward me, he exclaims with a deep laugh, "You think too much!" He always tells me I "think too much" when I am unhappy about something. I guess I should not dwell on the Family Planning director.

I tell Baba Mandaza about my project and the information I have collected so far. I wonder how sympathetic he is to the position of women in Zimbabwe. I am polite but straightforward in expressing my views to him, and though he does not argue with me, neither does he concur.

He changes the subject and asks me what I think of President Bush. I tell him I am opposed to many of President Bush's stances on both domestic and foreign issues. He knows that the United States will have a presidential election next month and asks if I will vote and who I would like to have as president. As I answer him, I watch his face. He listens to me with a thoughtful expression that compels me to think more about my words. He laughs when I tell him that I will not vote for President Bush. Although Zimbabwe is a democracy, the political system is corrupt to the point that President Mugabe is virtually guaranteed reelection if he chooses to run.

I remember that I have a copy of *Time* magazine that covers the current U.S. presidential campaign. I retrieve it from my room for him. He begins to look through it carefully. His gaze stops on a brief summary of occurrences in an East African country. The article is two paragraphs long with a picture of a starving child above it. The picture is the same size as the article.

Baba Mandaza points out, "You see, in the U.S.A., people think we starve in Africa. They do not think we can feed ourselves."

"Yes, most of the news in the U.S. about Africa seems to be about famine or violence."

"Why the U.S.A. does not write something else?"

I tell him that I wish newspapers in the U.S. covered Africa in a different way. He nods his head and looks at the article for several more minutes.

I will be moving out of the Mandaza house in a week. I have grown accustomed to the family and to their habits and schedules. I have acquired my own habits and schedules, too. Baba Mandaza and I have had some interesting conversations. We accept that our values diverge in significant areas. Only on a couple of occasions have I felt seriously offended by his sexist views.

I remember one time soon after I arrived here. I was in the kitchen getting a drink of water, it was dinner time, and Hannah was late returning from town. Baba was standing next to the stove, and I asked if he was making dinner. "Oh NO! I've boiled some chicken, but the rest NEEDS to be done by WOMEN!" He was serious, and somehow I managed to laugh off the comment. Somehow I didn't say everything I wanted to. I did mention, however, that "not in my opinion" does the rest of the work need to be done by women. He laughed. I wanted to scream.

Instead I retreated to my bedroom and wrote in my journal. It drove me crazy that a few moments later Hannah walked in the door and immediately began preparing dinner. Since that time, I have found more articulate ways of addressing the differences in our opinions. Still, Mr. Mandaza has made it clear to me that, as kind and thoughtful as he may seem, his views of women are unlikely to change.

My relationship with Hannah has been the best part of my experience in the Mandaza house. Not only have I always enjoyed talking with her, I have learned so much from her, too. My friendship with Hannah has also made it impossible for me to have a relationship with "the boys," Kenneth and Marcus. I have spoken with each one of them individually a handful of times. Kenneth has been most open to me, telling me about his teaching, and showing me photos of places he has seen in Zimbabwe that I have not yet visited. However, their disrespect for and mistreatment of Hannah make me avoid them except on a superficial level. Still, I do feel comfortable in this house and am grateful to the family for opening it to me.

I enter the kitchen and see that Hannah has already prepared dinner. I apologize for not coming to help her earlier. She never asks me to help her, so I have to pay attention to when she is in the kitchen. She almost constantly does housework, but she lets me help only in the kitchen. Sometimes when I leave my dirty laundry bag out, I later find her washing my clothes in the bathtub for me, and she even irons them. If we don't iron our clothes, we have to wait three days to wear them. Local flies, attracted to the damp cloth, lay eggs that burrow in the skin. Although I always tell Hannah I can do my own laundry, she doesn't seem to want me to clean. I think Amai Mandaza and I are the only ones who thank her for the work she does.

Hannah is a silent presence in the house. I don't think the boys even notice her much of the time. I have become so aware of her, however, that sometimes I tune out the rest of the household. As Hannah fills the plates, the boys and Mr. Mandaza come into the kitchen to get their dinner. The boys return to the living room, where Kenneth is grading papers and Marcus watches TV. Mr. Mandaza walks outside to where Hannah and I always eat.

We sit in chairs on the concrete path between the vegetable garden and the door to the kitchen. In the darkness, only the kitchen light illuminates our faces. Mr. Mandaza and I sit opposite each other and Hannah is to his left. He can't see her when he looks at me, but I can see both of them. I am not sure how, but we land on the topic of retirement. Baba and I joke about how bored we would be. Hannah is quiet, as she usually is in the presence of others. Eventually, I mention that I cannot imagine ever being bored. Baba laughs and agrees:

"Of course you would not be bored! There are always things for a woman to do! You must cook and clean. A woman can't be bored! It's the men who have to worry!"

I quickly respond, "I *meant* that I would not be bored because there always are books I want to read, places I want to go, or things I want to learn how to do! I did *not* mean that I'd be doing housework all the time! In fact, I think I *would* be bored if I were doing housework constantly!"

Baba laughs again, "Who else would do the housework if you were reading books all the time?!"

I look at Hannah, who has remained silent. She stares at the ground and sits very still. I wish she could venture her opinion. While Baba continues laughing about my impossible dreams, I keep watching Hannah. She lifts her large brown eyes and looks at me with a smile forming on her face. Then she glances at Baba and quickly looks down again. Baba changes the subject, but I still think about what he has just said to me, and Hannah still looks at the ground. At least someone understands.

## II  Learning: Beginning Independent Study

I push my way through the people on the sidewalk. Harare is always crowded during the week. When I am tired, it can seem as if everyone else is moving in the opposite direction to mine. Now is one of those times. I step off the sidewalk onto the street. The cars may be moving fast, but at least they are not quite as numerous as the people on the sidewalk.

I have started to research my independent study topic and have finally learned what baby dumping is. It means abandoning a newborn or infant and leaving him or her to die, or killing the baby and hiding the body. However, the main thing I have learned is that this is a challenging city in which to conduct research. I do not have access to a private telephone, so I am dependent on public telephones to contact potential interviewees. There are always long lines at public telephone booths, and frequently calls do not go through. If a call is unsuccessful, I have to go back to the end of the line to try again.

Many of the people I want to interview likewise do not have private telephones. Consequently, I have been walking all over the city trying to set up interviews. If the person I want to interview is far enough away that I must take a bus, I have to leave early in case a bus does not come, or comes much later than scheduled.

It has taken me a few days to adjust to this method of communication and travel. In the United States, logistics are less of a challenge because communications technology is more advanced than here. Both societies are alike, however, in tending to live according to the pace at which they can communicate and travel. Therefore, life in Harare moves at a more relaxed, fluid pace than life in U.S. cities. My challenge is to adjust my life and goals to meet the pace here. For example, if I set out to interview four people in one day, my chances of failure are great. If I aim to interview one person and make an appointment with one or two others, I am more likely to accomplish my goal.

My goal for today is to obtain some statistics on how many baby-dumping cases have gone through the courts. I want to know how widespread the problem is. I jump back up onto the sidewalk to avoid being crushed by a speeding bus, round the corner, and realize that I have found the High Court. Because everyone I ask gives me conflicting directions, I've been walking around Harare all day looking for it.

As I walk toward the front door of the building, a young man in a uniform comes chasing after me: "Wait! I need to look in your bag!" He examines my backpack full of notebooks, and I tell him I wish to speak with someone about infanticide cases. "Go to Room 1," he says.

I enter the building and locate Room 1 without much difficulty. I ask the first person I see for the statistics. "Go to Room 2." In this creatively organized building, Room 2 is not next to or even near Room 1. I eventually find it and see that it is the Registrar's office. I ask the Registrar about the statistics, and he promptly directs me to Room 17. Ten minutes later, through a courtyard and down a dark hallway, I locate Room 17 and ask, "Do *you* have statistics on baby-dumping and infanticide cases?"

"No. We do not keep that evidence."

"Do you mean to tell me that that information is nowhere in this court?"

"Try Room 25."

"Where is Room 25?"

The woman in Room 25 tells me to try the Magistrate Court, but she does not know where that court is. Before leaving the building, I collect several different opinions on where to find the Magistrate Court.

The court turns out to be on the other side of the city. When

I reach it, another fact-finding adventure begins.

"Go to Civil Case Enquiries." "Go to Criminal Case Enquiries." "Go to Room 287."

"Where's that?"

"Go to the librarian." "The librarian isn't in today." "Go to Room 210."

"Where's that?"

In Room 210, I see a man sitting at the desk, and I tell him why I'm here.

He responds, "Well, actually, this isn't my office. The person you are looking for isn't in." I can barely believe my bad luck, but he continues, "However, I think I may be able to help you."

He introduces himself as John Timmins and leads me to his office. He, like all of the people I have met in the courts, is white. I have seen more white people today than in my whole previous time in Zimbabwe. Mr. Timmins sits at his desk and hands me an article he recently wrote on the 1990 Infanticide Act. He tells me the names of some people who may have statistics I could use. Only after I have carefully written down all the names does he tell me that he has absolutely no idea where I might find any of these people.

Even though I ask him in five different ways who in the court has the statistics, he does not answer my question. Finally he breaks it to me that it is impossible to find statistical data in Zimbabwe and that people here are "paranoid" about letting outsiders see such information. I ask if there is anyone who will talk to me about it. "Go to Room 226."

In Room 226, I find a man who tells me that the only hope I have is to talk to someone in the Police Department. I don't bother to ask him where the Police Department is. I want to save that experience for tomorrow.

I wake up to see Hannah knitting on her bed. "Mangwanani," she greets me. "Mangwanani," I mumble, still blinking in the morning brightness. I see that it is just past 8 a.m., later than I have slept in a long time. I even went to bed early last night. Scouring the city for information must be wearing me out.

"Someone called for you last night on the telephone," Hannah casually mentions. Nobody ever calls me; none of my friends has a phone, and Baba Mandaza doesn't like us to use his telephone. I ask Hannah who it was.

"I don't know."

"Well, was it a man or a woman?"

"Oh, it was a woman. She said 'Baker,' and there is a meeting at nine today."

"What meeting at nine? And who is Baker?"

"I don't know. This woman said Baker and nine this morning."

Baker and 9 a.m. Mrs. Baker? Baker Street! Baker Street is where the Abandoned Babies' Committee (ABC) is located. I went there yesterday morning at the recommendation of a woman at ZWRCN. I left a note with the Mandazas' telephone number on it. Because I will be moving out of here in a few days, and then going on vacation, I want to contact the coordinator of ABC before I leave. I cannot believe this is happening: it is 8:15 a.m., I just woke up, I have a 9 a.m. interview in town and no questions prepared. I jump out of bed, throw on the nearest clothing, grab my notebook and run to the bus stop.

Fortunately, the bus arrives according to my schedule today. I have lost track of what the bus schedule is "supposed" to be. If it does not arrive, or arrives early or late, I consider it to be running according to its regular schedule. If it arrives when I need it to, it is running according to my schedule. Today it arrives at 8:30 a.m., the latest possible moment for me to reach ABC on time. I am also lucky to find a seat. I take out my notebook and jot down questions for my interview. Just when I am sure that I have not forgotten any important questions, we reach my stop.

I walk past some young men selling candy, cigarettes and oranges from boxes. I pass some men sitting on the sidewalk who call out, "Helloooo, Prinnnncess," "Come taalk to me, bay-bee." I find myself looking away from them as if I am the one who has done something wrong. The way they look at me makes me feel that I am in the wrong place, that this is their space, their sidewalk of maleness, and if I come here I am theirs to disturb as they please. Their look contains such a sense of power that I recoil in anger.

I want to lash out and make them shrivel in shame, make them see that I am a human being and deserve respect. But I never find the words. These men are so alien to me that I do not know what to say to them to make them understand that they are wrong. I have never felt more alienated from males and more defined by being female, than I have in Harare.

Their attitude only feeds my conviction that I and other women do not belong in the place they would like to put us. My conviction, however, is trapped in the maze of social, cultural and economic constraints against equality and respect for women. My quest to determine the reasons women dump their babies is a part of an effort to make my way through the maze. Whether the result is that a woman dump her baby, quits school, commits suicide, prostitutes her body, lacks a home, turns to drugs, or remains in an abusive marriage, the causes are likely to be similar.

I get past the men on the sidewalk, and they return to whatever they were doing before I distracted them. I press the ABC buzzer next to the gate, and the receptionist unlocks the iron gate and invites me to enter. I step inside and ask to speak with the coordinator, Mrs. Alice Mamutse.

The receptionist leads me into an office and introduces me to Amai Mamutse. Amai stands up behind her paper-laden desk and asks me to sit. I tell her who I am and that I am interested in interviewing her about her work. She says she would be happy to help. Her welcoming manner is encouraging, and the calm she exudes somehow assures me that she actually will help me. Amai Mamutse has bright eyes and energy in her voice. As she answers my questions, I begin to realize not only that baby dumping is a real problem but also that this woman knows what must be done to fix it. Finally my research can begin.

# III  Feeling: Hannah

I haven't been able to write letters for the past few weeks for lack of time and lack of will. My lack of will is what I've been trying to figure out. Perhaps I've needed some "alone time" to process what I am experiencing here. I've been in a sort of limbo, and it began four weeks ago when I moved out of the Mandazas' house and went on a trip. One gray day in the city of Bulawayo, I began to think about how no one in this country really knows me, and how I don't really know anyone in this country. At the same time, so much has happened that I feel incapable of explaining to anyone outside of this country.

My last night in Harare, the night before we left as a group for Bulawayo, something happened. Hannah was making dinner and I was in the kitchen with her. I love talking with her, so I followed her around the house. The older brother, Marcus, came in and they started talking in rapid Shona, not a word of which I understood. She began taking plates out from the cupboard to put food on, and I left the room to retrieve cookies I had brought home from town for the family. When I returned, Hannah was alone in the kitchen. She put food on all the plates except in the small white bowl she always reserves for herself; she put her bowl back in the cupboard.

"Why are you not eating, Hannah?"

"I'm not hungry."

"You need to eat. It's not healthy if you don't."

"No, I am not eating."

"What's wrong?"

"I don't feel well."

"Are you getting one of your bad headaches?"

"No."

"Is there anything I can do for you?"

"No."

We were both quiet for a moment. She had not looked at me since I returned to the kitchen.

"I think you should eat *something*. A little sadza at least. It'll make you feel better."

She refused to eat anything. I was upset because she is very thin and busy all the time, but every so often she does not eat dinner. I think it's unhealthy and I worry about her.

Breaking the silence we had fallen into, Hannah asked me what was wrong. I said I wanted her to eat. She consented to put a bit of sadza and muriwo in her bowl and came outside with me. We usually eat outside, behind the kitchen, while everyone else eats inside. Normally we talk with each other, but this time she said to me, "I don't want to be disturbed."

"OK, I won't disturb you." She ate a few bites of dinner, put her plate down and went inside. I left her alone until I finished my dinner. Then I went into our room and found her knitting on her bed. I asked her if she wanted to tell me what was wrong. "Yes, I will tell you. Later." "OK, tell me later."

I took out my school books and sat down on my bed to study. After about ten minutes, she told me she simply felt sick and that was all. I nodded and then continued looking through my books. After another few minutes, she said, "One of those boys hit me" and turned her face to show me where he'd hit her in the cheek. I could see a bruise forming on her face. There was no longer any air coming into my lungs and my eyes couldn't blink as I looked back at her brown eyes.

There was no reaction I could have. In the United States I could be angry and tell her that she "can't stand for this" and "we'll do something about it." I couldn't have that reaction here, though my insides were seething, and my only thought was needing to take Hannah out of her life. For lack of a better response, I asked her why he did it, though the answer didn't matter. "He was mad at me." We didn't discuss the reason any further. It was not necessary. The boys had threatened her with physical violence before when they felt she was not doing something right or fast enough, but this was the first time anyone had hit her. She never argues with them, no matter how absurd their accusations, because she is afraid of them. She said tonight Marcus was mad at her but she had "stayed silent."

I told her all the appropriate rhetoric about how it was not her fault. He was wrong. As the words fell off my tongue, I saw as well as she did that my message was virtually useless. Hannah understands the way her rights and life should be, and she understands what is wrong about the way they currently are, but that knowledge has no outlet in action for her.

Hannah then pulled out a number of books and pamphlets that a previous student had given her on violence against women, among other relevant issues. Hannah loves to read, and I am sure she has read all of them more than once. The way she was looking at them, though, made it clear that these progressive ideas just do not apply to her life. She has to stay in that house and tolerate abuse because there truly may be no other viable option for her. The handful of shelters in Zimbabwe for destitute women are perpetually full. Hannah has no means of supporting herself, especially without an education, with no relatives nearby to help her, and in an imperiled economy.

I told her that when she is married to her boyfriend, if he hits her she must leave. She sort of laughed, but she knew I was serious. I remarked that if I told her that someone hit me, she would tell me it was wrong and that I had to do something about it. She agreed. At that moment, the contrast between my position in life and hers became glaringly clear.

Soon Hannah left the room to clean up the dinner dishes. I left to go talk to Adam, another student who lives down the street. I needed to be with someone in whose presence I could release my sadness and anger. On my way out of the house, I saw Marcus eating one of the cookies I'd brought home for the family. The urge to choke him welled up so powerfully that I had to avert my eyes and leave the room as quickly as possible.

To some extent, it helped to talk with Adam, though he shared my feeling of helplessness. On the way home, I ran into Howard, a man I had met the previous morning who had a pet monkey. When I told Hannah about the monkey, she had said she wished she could have seen it. I persuaded Howard to bring his monkey to our house. I led Hannah outside very quietly so the boys would not get to see the monkey and surprised her with it. Her smile was enormous, and she asked endless questions about what it eats, where it sleeps, how old it is. Howard let her pet his monkey and hold the leash, and she laughed with delight at how the small monkey gripped onto her. When we finally went back inside the house, we didn't tell anyone about the monkey. It felt good to keep that experience to ourselves.

I insisted she tell Mr. or Mrs. Mandaza that their son had hit her. She replied that it would not make any difference. I was adamant, though I agreed with her. She finally agreed to tell Mr. Mandaza. We went to sleep, and when we woke up, she said she had dreamed about the monkey.

I left that morning for Bulawayo and have not been back yet, so I do not know how Hannah is. I have not been able to write a letter since that night. One reason is that I don't want people to use this as one of their "Perrin in Zimbabwe" or "sexism in Africa" stories. It is much more personal and also more global than that. Although the abuse occurred here and stems from aspects of this culture, similar abuse takes place everywhere in the world. I could not and would not make any excuses for what happened, but I still feel uncomfortable writing a letter about it.

Hannah shared her experience with me because she trusts me. I do not know how to share my part of the experience with anyone else. I do not know how to convey who Hannah is in her brightness, kindness, and dignity, what her life is like in its rigid drudgery, and how deeply the struggling country lacks sufficient services for women. How can I communicate to North Americans, who pride themselves on being independent and in control, how truly helpless I feel in this situation and how dependent Hannah is on that family?.

This limbo I have been in since that night is only partially from confusion; it is also from understanding. I understand how isolated Hannah is from resources available in the west, and how removed people in any place are from the personal realities of those elsewhere. I see myself on one side of an abyss, while all of my visions of a healthier world collect on the other side. Filling up the dark bottom are the realities I encounter each day. As they meet the ones I have stored from the U.S., they create a bubbling mixture that rises before me. I try to focus on one reality at a time, but the different ideas and experiences blend together or clash with one another until they are incomprehensible. I stare into this stew and realize I cannot possibly share my confusion with anyone. I can share the parts that stand out most distinctly, but must be content with letting the rest remain untold. I understand more than ever that I am here alone.

As that thought settles into my mind, I take out a pen and paper to write a letter. My thoughts wind themselves around the pen, and words form on the paper. It is possible to let others see some of what I see, and I must trust them to understand it for themselves.

# IV  Persisting: Baby Dumping — Searching for Answers

If I don't stop tapping my feet on the floor, I may wear a hole through it. I have been waiting here at ABC for Amai Mamutse all morning. Well, not "all" morning. Before coming here, I waited by a telephone for an hour for a call from a woman who was supposed to help me with my project. She never called. Then I went to the University of Zimbabwe to talk to an economics professor about post-independence economic pressures on women. He was not available. I looked for a professor in the Sociology Department who was also not there. Exams have just ended at the University, so the professors are hard to reach. I came here right after that because the receptionist had said that Amai Mamutse is usually in all day on Fridays. If she doesn't come in today, I'll sit here all day on Monday to make sure I see her.

My research is progressing at a snail's pace. Every day I wait and wait for people, for a bus, for a phone call. Every day I walk from one end of the city to the other, searching for information. Sometimes it seems that I am gathering a lot of information — until I go home and try to make sense of it. At that point, it usually becomes evident that all I have done is come up with more questions instead of finding the answers to my original ones.

At the beginning of this project, I was full of energy and drive to get to the root of the baby dumping problem. I developed an outline, wrote questions, made a list of places to go to find the answers, and started on my way. Still, every day I find myself taking one step forward and two steps back. There is something I am not doing right, and I do not know what it is.

I have never been more motivated to complete an assignment. This project feels important. It is relevant not only to Zimbabwe but to my personal concern for Hannah and other women like her. All day long, issues related to baby dumping flood my thoughts, and my mind spins with questions. I have never been more focused. I must figure out the right way to conduct research in Zimbabwe. Not a single day turns out as planned. Or maybe I should accept that there is little I can do differently; I must simply be patient and persevere.

Yesterday was a typically full and scattered day of research for me. I started out by perusing books at the University of Zimbabwe library, but only after proving I was "authorized" to enter the library. I met with the chair of the Sociology Department, who directed me to the School of Social Work. Miles away, at the School of Social Work, I met Mr. Chinaka, the principal. He was helpful and sent me to Rachel Makoni, a faculty member who he thought could help me.

After an improvised interview with Amai Makoni about social forces that might relate to unwanted pregnancies, I returned to ABC. There I pored through write-ups of the seminars they hold for women in the community. While walking back to the small hotel room I am living in with another student, I realized that although I had acquired interesting information, I had accomplished few of my goals for the day.

What I really want to do is interview some of the women who attend Amai Mamutse's "Day Center." I am waiting here to talk to Amai Mamutse and see if that is possible. ABC does not provide shelter, food, or financial assistance, but it does run three day centers. Amai says that the centers are for "occupational therapy" so women can learn skills to lift them from what she calls the "critical point" of desperation.

For example, at the day center in the high-density suburb of Kuwadzana, women learn sewing and baking skills that they hope to market. Amai makes sure to present the women who can read with books to inform them of their rights and options. She asks those women to share the information with the women who cannot read. I imagine that the center also provides a daily source of moral and emotional support for women who may have nowhere else to find it.

The door to ABC opens, but to my disappointment, Amai Mamutse is not the one opening it. Instead, it is the white woman with grey hair who runs Shelter Trust. I have not spoken with her yet, though I see her here frequently. Several years ago ABC created Shelter Trust, which operates in the office next to Amai Mamutse's. It runs two shelters for destitute women. Residents take classes in personal hygiene, baby care, hand and machine knitting and sewing.

I actually learned of Shelter Trust before realizing that it is located in this office. I read about it in articles at the Women's Action Group (WAG) a week ago. The name of the building that houses WAG is "Ivory House," a name I associate with "Ivory Tower," especially because WAG is located at the top of the white building. Although feminist organizations exist in Zimbabwe, they seem quite far from the consciousness of most women here.

Larger than that of ZWRCN or WiLDAF, WAG's office has several small rooms and one large work room. Tall bookshelves laden with logs of newspaper articles that track issues such as abortion, baby dumping, and laws pertaining to women's rights line the walls of the work room. WAG also has a significant collection of magazines and journals that deal with women's issues.

I flip through several of the carefully organized newspaper logs. Among the first articles I read are two on Shelter Trust. The shelters are perpetually full, indicating that they are needed. However, according to the articles, the public spoke out vehemently against the establishment of these shelters. Some parents believed that "their daughters would no longer listen to them, knowing that if they fell pregnant there was a refuge where they would be welcome." Another interviewee concurred: "it is justified for parents to reject their daughters when they fall pregnant."

While some interviewees expressed concern for parental authority, others focused on the issue of whether the women deserve a shelter. One asked "why the Shelter Trust was taking the trouble to look after pregnant girls who had been rejected by their own parents." To me, it makes sense that Shelter Trust is connected with the Abandoned Babies' Committee because ABC is devoted to helping destitute women and their babies, regardless of social stigma or financial improbability. Instead of worrying about the accepted ways of dealing with women in desperate situations, ABC addresses the women's basic needs in a constructive manner.

The articles opposing the shelters amaze me because the fearful and angry responses seem so contrary to the logic I use when looking at the issue. Our "logical" reasoning differs, maybe because we come from different cultures and subscribe to different moral structures. When I take a step back, I understand the opposition in terms of what I have learned of the Shona view of women and family. I also see that the "traditional" Shona perspective is not too different from conservative U.S. perspectives. My primary concern is for the girls and women who are left hopeless and helpless when shelters do not exist. I also become fearful and angry at the thought of girls and women being demonized because they become pregnant.

As I sit tapping my feet and waiting for Amai Mamutse, I look over a study of infanticide done in 1986 by a "sub-committee" of ABC. The authors write that a primary limitation of their study is that they could not obtain information from the courts. They ultimately managed to acquire cassette tape recordings of court cases and listened to twenty of them in order to extract some statistical information.

Because I have also been unable to obtain information from the courts, I copy down statistics from this report for my own use. In the U.S., I grew accustomed to the accessibility of government statistics when I wrote research papers. I have also spent hours in this office copying down information verbatim because there is no copy machine, something else I took for granted in the U.S.

Reading about the difficulty the researchers had in obtaining information, I feel relieved. It helps to know that I am not the only one who has had this problem. My project agenda and good organizational skills will not take me far in Zimbabwe. I need to adapt my expectations of myself and my project to coincide with what I know to be possible here. Because I am new to research here, my expectations will need to be low. The hardest part about having to lower my expectations is that my desire to know the answers to my questions remains strong.

The report describes the circumstances of the typical baby-dumping case in Zimbabwe. It involves a rural, unmarried, twenty-one-year-old woman with minimal education. The father of her child rejects her and disappears soon after he learns she is pregnant. Because she believes her family will refuse to support her, she hides her pregnancy from them. "She believes her situation to be desperate" and is unaware of possible social service assistance. She keeps the baby's due-date a secret and ultimately gives birth alone. Immediately after giving birth, she kills the baby and hides the body, which is found shortly thereafter. "She is likely to spend seven months on remand...and eventually receives a prison sentence of about three and one-half years."

As I read through this description, my first reaction is horror at the thought of how the woman must feel as she kills her baby and after she has done so. Then I feel horror at how she must have felt before she killed her baby. I do not believe that she is an evil person; most likely she feels there is no other way for her to survive. I try to imagine the socioeconomic forces that would explain why the woman has received only a minimal education, why the baby's father does not feel compelled to take any responsibility for the baby, why the woman's family would refuse to support her, and why she is unaware of the social services available to her. The answers to these questions must lie at the root of the baby-dumping problem.

I look up from my reading to see Amai Mamutse finally coming through the door. I have been waiting for two and a half hours. She greets me and says she can talk with me after she makes a quick phone call. I am happy to wait until she makes ten phone calls now that I know where she is and that I will definitely be talking with her today. I settle back into my chair and continue reading the report.

In the Subcommittee's examination of sixty-two infanticide cases in which a new-born infant is killed, the charge is murder or attempted murder. In all but two of the cases, the charge is murder. Fifty-three women were found guilty of murder, six were found guilty of concealment, two were found guilty of attempted murder. Only one woman was found not guilty. For the fifty-three women convicted of murder, suspended sentences were included. The average term of "effective imprisonment" is three years and one month. As I read through the guilty verdicts, what is most striking is that every one of these women is also a victim.

The report lists factors that influenced the length of the sentences the women received. The factors include the emotional state of the accused, her age, previous births, dependents, manner of killing, education and employment, and support. Although a woman's emotional state is considered an influential factor, a psychiatric report was used in only three cases. Moreover, her emotional state was considered only in that the court assumes that no reasonable woman would commit this crime.

The judgment is more harsh if a woman is over twenty-one years of age, has had previous births, has dependents, and if she used an active manner of killing (as opposed to simply leaving her baby to die). Her level of education and her employment status do not have a significant impact on the sentencing; however, I imagine that these two factors have a significant bearing on the reason she chose to dump her baby. Similarly, whether she claims to have any financial or emotional support also has very little bearing on her sentencing.

The patriarchal nature of the court process is remarkable. In 73 percent of the cases, the accused was the sole woman in the courtroom. Only twice was the state represented by a female prosecutor, and only eight of the sixty-two times was there a female defense attorney. Most significantly, the father was named in 61 percent of the cases but was called to give testimony in only four cases. This fact in particular seems to reveal the lack of responsibility men are expected to take for the children they bring into the world.

The male participants in the court proceedings demonstrated an ignorance of or insensitivity to the nature of the birth process. For example, the report cites that "In one case, the Prosecutor asked the woman whether she had experienced any pain while giving birth. The judge criticized the same woman for falling asleep several hours after the birth." As I read through the report, I can think only that the court process is symbolic of a general lack of understanding of and sensitivity to the needs of pregnant women and single mothers in Zimbabwe.

Just as I finish reading the report, Amai Mamutse stands in her doorway and beckons me into her office. I sit in a large, old leather chair across from her desk as she shuffles some papers around. When she finishes, she smiles and asks, "How can I help you today?" Just having someone offer to help me makes my project feel less daunting. "I would like you to tell me more about the sort of women who come here," I answer.

She speaks with a strong Shona accent, and sometimes I have trouble understanding her words. She tells me that she screens every woman who comes to her in order to determine whether the woman has been "chased away" and has nowhere to stay, and to find out the age of the baby. ABC does not handle cases in which the child is more than two years old. It is when a woman is at the "critical point" before dumping her baby, Amai Mamutse says, that she usually needs basic support, such as money for food or clothing.

Another important factor, she explains, is that most women are not aware of their legal rights under the Legal Age of Majority Act (LAMA) and Maintenance law. Women who are unaware of these laws understand their situation in terms of customary law rather than current civil law. Before LAMA was passed in 1982, black Zimbabwean women were perpetual minors under the authority of their fathers and then their husbands. There was a separate law for white women. LAMA established that every person is a major at the age of eighteen. For the first time, all women had access to the courts and to private bank accounts, among other crucial links to independence.

The 1987 Maintenance law gives a child's parents legal responsibility to provide for the child within their means. They are responsible regardless of whether the child is illegitimate or legitimate, and whether the parents are divorced, cohabitating, or separated. If the parents do not live together, the parent who lives with the child is entitled to receive maintenance from the other parent.

Theoretically, both of these laws grant increased independence to women. When women do not know about the laws, however, the laws do not help them. Furthermore, if the child's father is unemployed or cannot be located, the child's mother is left with the burden of caring for the baby alone. There are no provisions for women in the event that the child's father does not contribute to the maintenance of the child. It does not matter if she is unemployed, as most women here are, or if she also would like to "disappear" as the father may have. As the mother, she is responsible for the life of the child.

Because it is nearly impossible for most women in Zimbabwe to be financially independent of their families, Amai Mamutse tries hard to reconnect women with their families. When the family is local, Amai visits them to arrange a reconciliation. If the family lives farther away, she contacts the regional police to handle the matter. She usually tries to persuade the family to take their daughter home.

When a family has physically threatened a daughter, Amai intervenes and tries to mediate with the parents. If a woman asks that her family not be contacted, Amai will strongly urge her to change her mind. She feels it is extremely important that the woman be reconciled with her family. One explanation she gives for wanting the reconciliation is that all employers ask for an applicant's family history and living situation. If a woman is disconnected from her family, the employer may distrust her and not hire her.

Amai tells me that one reason many parents react negatively toward a destitute daughter involves a cultural belief that her baby's blood contains foreign ancestral spirits. Traditionally children live in their father's home. If a destitute woman's baby happens to die while living with his/her mother's family, the baby's spirits may cause great problems for that family. Amai Mamutse explains that it is for this reason that adoption is generally unacceptable to the Shona people.

I am fascinated by what Amai Mamutse has told me, but we have been talking for an hour and the receptionist keeps bringing more papers to Amai's desk. I do not want to overstay my welcome. Amai and I arrange a date for me to come to the Kuwadzana Day Center with her to interview some of the women who attend. I am grateful for her generosity in giving me time and in sharing her knowledge. As I leave the office, I find myself wondering more about Amai Mamutse herself, and about her personal reasons for doing this work. I hope I have a chance to get to know her better.

This morning has been full of disappointments. I went to the University of Zimbabwe to speak with a professor during her office hours, which begin at 9:00 a.m. I arrived at 8:15 a.m. to make sure I was first in line. I had written out detailed questions and reviewed them so many times that I almost memorized them. She did not show up. Nobody I asked had any idea where she might be or if she might arrive later. I went home to call the Ministry of Information to ask where I might find statistical information on Zimbabwe. The man who answered the phone would not help me, which makes me wonder what a "Ministry of Information" is for.

My disappointment comes from how much I have grown to care about this project. Each time I talk to Hannah, I tell her what I have been learning about women in Zimbabwe and the connection to baby dumping. I want her reaction. With each new issue I introduce, she looks at me as though I am telling her her own life story. I see that the pressures leading a woman to dump her baby are the same pressures that women all over this country feel. Not all have unwanted pregnancies, and not all who do dump their babies, but the stresses exist regardless.

Last weekend, I stopped by the Mandazas' house to visit. Hannah was the only one home. She was on her hands and knees polishing the floor in the living room, and though she was humming to the radio, the humming was not joyful. She looked up at me and her face spoke of unhappiness, unfulfillment. I had burst into the room full of energy and vitality because of my project. She was downcast. We both felt the contrast.

She sat at the table with me and I told her about the latest developments in my project. She looked interested and amused as I spoke. I asked her why she looked that way and she told me that she was interested in what I had learned. I think it was my intensity that amused her. She cannot imagine feeling this way because she has never had the opportunity to challenge herself intellectually. While I have been immersing myself in issues that inspire me, she has been inside the house cleaning and cooking.

As Hannah and I reached agreement over the many sources of pressure on Zimbabwean women, I told her that I think she should be researching with me. She is an insider, I am an outsider. Together, I think we would be a good team. "I cannot," she said. She does not have the time or the freedom in the Mandaza family to take time off for research. She said it is better if I do it. "You are smart," she said. It doesn't make any difference that I think she is smart, too.

What I am learning about women in Zimbabwe is also teaching me about women in the United States and elsewhere. I never thought carefully about the reasons so many women in the world end up desperate and destitute. I paid more attention to debate over ways in which the government could "fix" the problems by means of laws or programs. Because Zimbabweans are generally less aware of the government than are people in the United States, my research has led me to pay attention to other factors influencing society. I find that what lies beneath society's surface is much more complex and relevant to the reality of women's lives than are laws and public policy.

My slow progress in the research is frustrating because this is the first time in my life I have had the opportunity to become so deeply involved in an issue - the first time I have not had other classes or commitments to prevent me from becoming as immersed in a subject as I want to be. What I want is to learn as much as possible about why baby dumping occurs. Unfortunately I have only a month to research and write the project. What is possible to learn is far less than what I want to know.

I am now heading into town to try to find the police station. Fortunately it is not too difficult to find, and a considerate man just inside the door helps me. He directs me to the Officer Commanding Central. I do not know exactly what the "Officer Commanding Central" does, but he looks important dressed in a uniform and wearing a stern expression on his face. I explain that I am a student doing a project on infanticide, mostly through the Abandoned Babies' Committee, and would like some information on cases that come through this station.

"Do you have a work permit for this research?" Because our Directors told us never to use the word "research" in Zimbabwe as it implies an official study requiring various official permits, I was careful not to use the word in introducing myself. He must not have heard me correctly.

I respond, "This is not a *research* project. I am a student and it is my personal interest."

"This is not true. The Police Department is a government body and if you want government information, you give me a permit from your embassy to introduce you." His voice has an angry edge and his eyes are cold.

"I am sorry, but this is only personal interest, so my government would not find it important. I am only here for a short time, and it would take a long time to obtain a permit simply to look into my personal interest." I hand him the two letters of introduction from my directors that explain that my project is not "research."

"These letters are addressed to NGOs," he says, standing up forcefully. "They do not apply to me. If your research is only personal interest, then you should not need government information."

He does hear me. He looks at me as though I am lying to him. The more upset I become, the greater is his pleasure in upsetting me. I try two more times to explain to him what I am trying to do. Each time his response contains more anger, more venom. When I plead with him to stop and listen to me for a moment, his voice rises practically to a yell. I stand up to leave, and as I reach the door I turn to him:

"First of all, you are wrong. You are not listening and you are not hearing me. Second of all, you are treating me with disrespect, and that is not appropriate."

There is so much more I want to scream at this man, but instead I leave. I seem to have absorbed his anger, though, because I cannot even bring myself to respond to the first person who greets me as I walk down the dark hallway to the exit. Once outside the building, I glance at the letters from my directors. Neither one says anything about "NGOs," as he had said. He really was not listening.

Although he didn't know me, his treatment of me felt personal. When he looked at me, I felt as if he was seeing something detestable. Was it my white skin (instead of black like his), my being foreign, my being female? Which offense was it that provoked his reaction? I did not have a chance with him; his feelings toward me felt immediate. Never before have I been treated with such vehement disgust by a total stranger. I wonder if this is what being the object of racism or of undisguised sexism feels like. Whatever its name, it is a horrible feeling.

All I want to do after the Police Department disaster is go home and not talk to anybody. However, I am supposed to meet Amai Mamutse at ABC at 1:00 p.m. to go with her to the day center. I arrive there straight from the Police Department at 12:00 p.m., still upset by the experience. I decide to use the hour to write in my fieldwork journal and collect my thoughts for interviewing the Day Center women.

The next time I look at my watch, it is 1:30 p.m. By 2:45, it becomes clear that Amai Mamutse is not going to come to the office. She must have forgotten our meeting and gone straight to the center this morning. I call a few people on the Board of Directors to see if they know where the center is, but the only one I can reach does not know. I have spent from 8:15 a.m. to 3:00 p.m. having my hopes crushed. The only bright side is that I have enough money to take a cab home so that I do not have to battle this city for one more minute.

Sharon Maberly is the University of Zimbabwe professor who lectured to our group on the Shona family and culture during orientation. I arranged a meeting with her to ask her some questions related to my project, and she was enthusiastic about helping me. I sit on her couch while she goes to the kitchen to get us water. Sharon was born in Zimbabwe and is one of the whites in the country who is sensitive to the blacks and supportive of their independence. She had been married to a black man from Britain, and tells me that while they were married, others assumed that he was the native Zimbabwean, and that she was from Britain.

When she joins me, she glances at the notebook in my lap and asks how my research is going. I tell her that I have had difficulty finding statistics, and she immediately rattles off three places I should go to find them. I cannot believe that what I have spent two weeks looking for has just fallen into my lap. I wonder what else she can tell me.

I explain what my project is about and she asks me to describe the information I have gathered thus far. When I mention my interest in learning more about how sex education and family planning programs work here, she raises an eyebrow. "I can tell you a bit about that," she says. I came here for answers to a few questions about the Shona family, but I think I may receive much more than that.

Sharon leans into the corner of her couch and her casual demeanor helps me relax. She begins to explain that the Shona culture's view of contraception creates a barrier to effective family planning by linking contraception and immorality. If a married woman uses contraceptives, her husband commonly believes she is cheating on him. Moreover, he probably assumes that it is the man's role to decide when to have children. A woman who uses contraception before marriage is considered "spoiled" because she is not a virgin. She may also be considered a prostitute.

As a result of these stigmas, an unmarried woman may worry that if she uses birth control, she is admitting that she is "loose." If she does not use birth control and becomes pregnant, she may console herself and her family by explaining her sexual activity as a "mistake" or a product of "true love." Such excuses tend to be more socially acceptable than to be part of a conscious plan to engage in premarital sex.

Sharon also tells me that while aunts and uncles of children in villages used to be responsible for teaching them sex education, urban migration has weakened such family systems. Many members of families live separate lives, some living in rural areas and some in the city. The break-up of the family has affected many customs, including that of aunts and uncles teaching sex education. Sex education in rural areas used to be a cultural norm, but now children may have no ready source of such information.

In the course of her own research, Sharon asked girls from Mount Pleasant School to say who had spoken to them about puberty issues, and "over 50 percent of the girls interviewed so far said, 'nobody's spoken to me.'" The Ministry of Education surveyed Mount Pleasant School, which takes students from high-density areas, and over 90 percent of the students said they wanted to have sex education taught in schools; over 90 percent of the parents said they did not approve. Parental attitudes contribute to the reason why the majority of women do not learn of birth control until they have already had one child.

As Sharon speaks, I scribble down as much of the information as I possibly can. I almost cannot focus on what she says because I am so amazed that she is giving me information I have spent weeks looking for all over Harare. I did not come to meet with Sharon thinking she would provide it, yet here it is.

Part of what has made my research difficult is that I have been able to locate neither written information on my topic nor the right people to interview. Listening to Sharon, I think of Africa's oral tradition of passing along history, information and stories. Sharon's contribution is like water flowing through the roots of a tree to many branches. As one branch of a tree of people talking, I wonder if this process might be a variation on the oral tradition.

Learning in this way takes patience. Personal exchanges offer a more social method of obtaining information than reading books in a library, and they are much less formal than holding an interview with a list of questions in my hand. Personal exchanges can be difficult, like my experience at the Police

Department, but they also give the issues a more personal meaning.

Personal meaning is the core of my project. The pressures on women that lead to baby dumping come from social and cultural systems that have deep personal meaning to the people involved. The systems' roots in personal meaning are what make them powerful. Similarly, the economic pressures on women and the governmental role in their lives stem from deeply held beliefs about the value of women and family.

This project has personal meaning to me. Through my research, I am learning the reality of what it means to be a woman in Zimbabwe. Because the issues are global, I feel that I also am connecting with the lives of women all over the world. Most important to me, I am forging a bond with Hannah and beginning to understand her life.

I believe it is an injustice that Hannah lives as she does. I believe it is unfair that someone as bright and curious as she cannot finish school and use her mind, as I know she craves to do. I feel that it is wrong that she must suffer the threat of abuse at home and have nowhere else to go, and that she must spend each day laboring for two young men who make her miserable and do not respect her.

Not only have I accepted her current position in life, I have accepted that at present she has no choice. However, before I leave Zimbabwe, I need to understand why her life is what it is. I want to know that there are traceable reasons for her condition and that they can be addressed. I want to know that it is not inevitable for women to live as she does. I want to know that there are choices to be made along the way and an opportunity for change in the future.

Feeling that I have been more productive today than I was all week, I decide to take the rest of the day off to spend an afternoon appreciating Harare without having any obligations. When I am not trying to accomplish something, I love walking around this city. A vibrancy radiates from the people walking down the sidewalks, from their smiles, their hard work, their willingness to greet a stranger. I imagine that every person I see has a fascinating history. I pass the Ethnomusicology building and decide to stop in and see if Cris is available. This would be a nice afternoon for a drum lesson.

Cris is happy to play drums with almost anyone, so he picks up a three-foot-tall drum and leads me outside. There are several other Ethnomusicology students sitting on the steps, and we sit down with them. I did not expect my first drum lesson to be in the presence of all these musicians, but they are friendly. Before I even begin to play, they laugh gleefully at the sight of me with the drum. I don't ask what they think is so funny.

Cris starts me with a rhythm so simple that I wonder if I should be insulted. One beat on the rim of the drum with my four fingers, and two quick beats in the center of the drum with an open hand. He tells me to continue my rhythm while he plays a variation. As we drum together, the other musicians begin to tap and hum and whistle in time. I have to concentrate hard on my simple beat in order not to become completely absorbed in the sounds they make. Cris smiles as if nothing in the world is better than making music on the steps in the shade of afternoon. As my mind lets go of thought and becomes conscious only of music, I feel the same smile forming on my face.

# V  Returning: Wachikwa III

I think Melissa and I have been waiting for about two hours for the bus to Wachikwa. When we arrived at the Mbare bus terminal at 10:00 a.m., it was already blazing hot and no seats in the shade were left. It took us a long time to figure out where to wait for our bus, but still we have not figured out when it is scheduled to arrive. So we wait. In the hot sun we drink Coca-Cola because it is cool, and we hope that we are waiting in the right place.

I look forward to seeing my Amai and Baba and to being away from the city. I try to focus on an image of Wachikwa and ignore the heat and the possibility that we are not waiting in the right place. Minutes are ticking away into hours, and annoyance at the uncertainty of the bus system starts to eat away at my excitement. Finally we find a place to sit in the shade next to a woman and a couple of live chickens. After settling in, I buy a cherry-flavored Freeze-It. As the sweet ice begins to cool my mouth and my skin enjoys the respite from the sun, I feel significantly more patient.

A couple of hours later, three buses cough and rumble into the terminal as hoards of people swarm toward them. At the sight of the throng separating into three sections, I feel compelled to pick one crowd and rush with it toward a bus. However, I do not know which bus is ours. I find myself feeling increasingly panicked as different people give us different responses to the question, "Which bus goes to Wachikwa?" Ultimately we choose the bus to which we have been directed by the most people. We wedge our bodies onto a bus that is bursting with people, produce, and a chicken or two.

The ride is bumpy and swelteringly hot. People stare at Melissa and me, and a few ask us where we are going and why. Miraculously a small space opens up in a seat right next to where we are standing. Gratefully, Melissa and I both stuff our bodies into it. I remember when I first took a bus to Wachikwa and it was just as hot, crowded and bumpy then as it is this time. I recall having slept through the whole ride, sleep being the least disruptive means of escape that I could come up with. This time, however, I am alert, imagining Wachikwa and anticipating how good it will feel to be there.

The bus stops do not seem to be marked. Frequently it comes to a halt at a place without houses or people anywhere in sight, and a passenger disembarks. I hope I do not miss my "stop." We move through an area that looks familiar but only because of the huts and open space. Most of the country looks like this, so I cannot be sure that we are anywhere near Wachikwa. Melissa and I ask the people behind us if they know where we should get off and they simply say, "soon." They are right: shortly thereafter, we catch sight of the Kyandere Primary School buildings. The bus stops as we call out to the driver. Because we are sitting in the back of the bus, it takes several minutes for us to make our way through the people and goods in the aisle. I cannot help stepping on some lettuce and grain as well as on some feet. The bus driver revs the engine, preparing to pull back onto the road, and we yell for him to wait. Finally we end up outside the bus with our backpacks securely on our backs. The bus jolts away, churning dust in our faces.

I turn around and am greeted by the familiar sight of the school, the headmistress's home, the chickens, the wide open space and the distant mountains. For a moment I simply stand still and absorb the sight, the clean air, the quiet. It is so quiet here that I can hear the chickens clucking across the schoolyard and leaves rustling in the slightest breeze. In Harare, individual sounds are lost in the city noise. Here everything feels hushed.

Melissa and I part to go in search of our families and surprise them. We decided only last week that we would come here and there was no way to let them know of our plans. I look forward to surprising everyone. It is evening and the sun is setting behind me. Shades of scarlet spread across the sky as I walk toward my Amai and Baba's home. In the hazy light of dusk, I see my Amai about one-hundred yards from me herding goats across the path to the house. At that moment, she looks up and recognizes me instantly. She calls out, "Tonderai!" and begins running toward me. I answer, "Amai!" With the sunset and the goats and my Amai running across the yellow field toward me, I feel as if I am in a movie.

When she reaches me, her smile is bigger than I remember it and her eyes are bright. She showers me with questions about why I am here and repeats how happy she is to see me. She takes my arm and leads me to the house. After she puts my backpack in my bedroom, we tend to the goats. Then we go to the kitchen hut, and she builds a fire. She tells me that Baba will be home soon, and we both laugh as we imagine how surprised he will be.

As she fills me in on how the crops are holding up to the drought, we hear Baba walking up the path to the kitchen. He enters, not yet noticing me, and I greet him with, "Manheru, Baba!" He turns, and automatically begins his response to the greeting, "Manheru...*Tonderai*?" Amai and I laugh as we watch him register the fact that I am here. He laughs with us at his surprise, and tells me how happy he is that I have come back. "Ndinofara," they both keep saying, "I am happy."

As Amai prepares dinner, I offer them gifts I have brought from Harare. I brought sugar, which they happen to be almost out of, matches, and shampoo for Amai. Last time she asked if she could have my shampoo. She had said that her head itches, so I brought medicated shampoo from the pharmacy in Harare.

Throughout the dinner of sadza and muriwo, I find myself forgetting that I have been living in Harare and that I will be returning there shortly. Life here already feels normal to me again. We talk a lot, making our usual U.S.-Zimbabwe comparisons. We discuss the average age at marriage, kinds of plows, and cities. I begin to tell them about my research project, but I hesitate. It feels like an insult to talk to them about the hardship of women who abandon their babies when Amai and Baba wish more than anything that they could have a child. They do not pursue the conversation, so I let it go. Amai and Baba's longing for a child is as real as the suffering of the women with unwanted babies.

They say they have a lot of plowing to do, and I ask if I can do it with them. "Oh, Tonderai! It is hard and we wake up verrry early!" Baba tries to discourage me, but I can tell he likes the idea of teaching me how to plow. I insist that I don't mind waking up early, although I have to hide a wince when they mention the 4:00 a.m. start. They like to start in plenty of time before it becomes too hot for them and for the cow. They agree to include me in tomorrow morning's plowing as long as I go to bed early.

Shortly after dinner, they usher me off to bed. I sit down on the familiar itchy woolen blanket on the bed and light a candle. After I hear Amai and Baba go to bed, I open the window to let in some fresh air. Hopefully, Amai won't notice it when she wakes me in the morning. I take out my journal to write but find that I have little to say. I am simply relaxed and content. I walk outside and am surprised by the darkness. Last time I was here, the moonlight illuminated everything. There is no moon tonight, and though the land around me is enveloped by darkness, the sky is a blanket of starlight, and I would be content to sit outside in the warm night and look up at it for hours. However, I did promise that I would get sleep tonight so that I will have energy for plowing in the morning. I retreat into my room and fall asleep quickly.

"Tonderai?" I hear Amai's hesitant voice from outside my door and look at my watch. It's 4:30 a.m., a half-hour later than they had said we would wake up. "Mangwanani, Amai! I'll be right there!" I try to sound as if I have been awake and ready to go for hours instead of sleeping like a log. She disappears into the kitchen hut. I hurry because we are starting late, and I suspect they planned that for my sake. I step outside and stop for a moment to take in the sight of the peach sunrise, the gentle, cool morning air, the birds, the stillness, the perfection. Baba and I greet each other as he hurries off to get a cow.
 When Baba returns, Amai and I are waiting at the plot of land. It looks pretty small to me, and I wonder if they picked it in order to teach me how to plow. Baba and Amai harness the black cow, and Baba shouts at it to start walking. As he guides the plow through the dirt in a perfectly straight line, he calls to me over his shoulder, "Come, you must watch!" Because everything he does looks natural, I don't know what to focus on. The cow pulls the plow and Baba guides it in a straight line. Amai walks along and shouts at the cow if it begins to stray off course. She holds a long whip in her hand, that she periodically lashes next to the cow. After Baba has completed several rows, Amai takes over. She is just as assured and competent as Baba, and I am impressed by her strength.
 Then it's my turn. I take hold of the heavy plow and Baba shouts for the cow to go. The cow is probably not moving at the speed of light, but it begins to feel that way to me as I struggle to control the motion of the unwieldy plow. The plow wobbles back and forth in my arms, and Baba tells me, "Lean forward! Push down! Lean back!" We make it to the end of the row and have to laugh at the neatly wavy line I have created. I try again, and while this time I have slightly more control, I cannot help feeling that my efforts to help will only result in more work for

Amai and Baba. They seem to be having fun, though, and are very patient with me. I imagine that they will no longer look at me in disbelief when I say that my "Amai in the U.S.A." does not plow.

We plow for a couple of hours and manage to finish the whole plot. By the end I perform much more adeptly, though I probably would not win any plowing awards. We decide that my contributions add an artistic flair to the rows. Amai frees the cow from the wood and metal contraption, and Baba leads it back to the other cattle. Amai and I proceed to wash last night's dinner dishes. After we bathe, it is time for breakfast. As I sit with Amai and Baba in the kitchen hut, I feel settled into a routine.

After breakfast, Amai and I wash dishes again, clean the kitchen hut, and collect water. She tells me the well is quite low because of the persistent drought, which is more devastating than she wants me to know. Farms have dried up, water in wells drops lower and lower, cattle have died. In many areas, women must walk miles to find a source for water. In an economy that is based on agriculture, the scope of the devastation is huge. Amai prefers not to dwell on these thoughts with me.

To entertain ourselves, Amai and I take pictures of each other doing different tasks. We use almost a whole roll of film because there is a lot to do. When we finish our tasks, Amai and I walk over to Amai Moyana's house to visit. She has already heard that I am in the village and is all set to fill me in on the recent events at Kyandere Primary.

As Amai Moyana launches into a description of her new goals for the school, the feeling that I am only a weekend visitor here slowly flows through me. Earlier, I was participating by teaching in the school. Then I was involved in what was happening. Now I am a visitor and can only hear about what is happening, and when I leave tomorrow I probably will not return for a long time. I leave Zimbabwe in less than a month and do not expect to return to Wachikwa in that time. While listening to Amai Moyana, I also watch her and this room, the tea cups, the flies. This weekend is the beginning of my goodbye.

Throughout the weekend, all my senses seem overly sharp. Each face I see, each song I hear, everything that happens, my senses latch onto. I do not like this feeling but am unable to ignore it. Each sense is trying to capture parts of my experience in this village, and each one is working independently. My eyes lock onto the sight of my Amai cooking dinner, my skin memorizes the evening breeze, my ears ring with the sounds of animals. Because I am so acutely aware of each sense, I am not experiencing this weekend as a whole. Every experience is divided into parts.

I will not be back in this village for a long time, and I know that some part of my brain is asking my senses to record this experience into memory. But I do not want to remember merely a song, or the tartness of an unripe mango. I want to remember this experience in its entirety. Perhaps, there is no way to do that. I am beginning to understand that I cannot take this entire experience with me. I can take it only in parts. I might remember sitting under a mango tree with Melissa and the women from the women's club as they make clay pots. But I might not recall what we talked about or who told what jokes. When I go away, I will have to leave something behind.

The women are chattering away and pulling out drums as we wait for the bus to take Melissa and me back to Harare. When I said goodbye to Baba this morning, he said over and over again how happy he is that I came to visit them. He and Amai insist that they will visit me in Harare before I leave. I do not expect them to come, because of the expense of the bus ride, but I appreciate the thought. Amai has been standing beside me with a huge smile on her face all morning.

One woman begins to hum, and the others pick up the tune. Someone raps on a drum, and gradually we all begin to sing and laugh and dance. I do not know how much longer we have before the bus arrives, and I do not know how much of this song I will remember once I reach Harare. But in this moment of laughter, music and movement, I finally feel complete.

# Excerpt 4

# VI Questioning: Baby Dumping — Finding Clarity

I'm on the eleventh floor of a building on Second Street that I have walked by countless times before. I wish I had known that this building houses the World Bank Library and that the library has statistics and other people's analyses of women in Zimbabwe. Sharon sent me here, and I am grateful to her. I had been looking high and low for statistics on women. I may have found a gold mine, even though there is not a ton of material. Not to mention that the room is air conditioned, and this must be the first time I have felt such cool air in months. This place feels like an oasis of information and cool air.

I sit at one of the long tables and read through World Bank and UNICEF documents on women and education and employment. I am encouraged by the fact that much of what I read does not come as a surprise to me. Instead, it confirms or expands on thoughts I have developed in the rest of my research, causing me to believe that what I have gathered is useful and that my understanding of the information is sound. I am relieved to find documentation to support my perspective, though the importance of this kind of "documentation" is not as significant here as it is in the West.

Right now I focus on women's educational and employment opportunities in Zimbabwe. I believe that much of the cause for baby dumping is that women do not expect to be able to support themselves and their babies financially. In the material I am reading, I note that a woman's ability to participate in formal employment is determined largely by her level of education and skills. Unfortunately women do not always have access to education or skills training. As one World Bank study shows, "When resources are short, parents in Zimbabwe...prefer to send their sons rather than their daughters to secondary school."

The parents' bias stems largely from cultural measures of female versus male worth. If a man marries a good wife who gives him many children, he enriches his parents' family. If he appears able to support such a woman, he is more likely to be granted marriage to her. His future employment and ability to support a family are related to his level of education. Therefore, parents send their sons to school partly to increase the likelihood that the sons are granted marriage to a desirable woman.

Although an education does make a woman more attractive to potential suitors, it is her apparent ability to bear many children and to be a "good wife and mother" that is most important. Therefore, as some Zimbabweans say, her value can be measured more by the width of her hips, and her skills at cooking and housework, than by her level of education. With such lack of support for girls' education, I am not surprised that the dropout rate of females exceeds that of males at every level of school.

I cannot help but imagine myself in the position of these girls. How different I might be had my education not been encouraged and supported. I contemplate the differences between myself and Hannah, and it is clear to me that in many ways we are products of our societies. In my family and community, it has always been assumed and expected that I will do well in school and pursue a career of my choice. In Hannah's family and community, it is assumed that the only thing she need aspire to be is a good wife and mother, regardless of her other personal interests or desires. Who would I be if my family and community had assumed something else for my life? Who would Hannah be? Both of us share a basic curiosity about the world around us and we enjoy reading, learning, and discussing. I will graduate from college in a year and a half. Hannah is several years older than I, has not finished secondary school, and for years has not even attended school.

Could I have focused on school and succeeded while everyone around me was assuming that school was not a high priority for a girl? I think of my high school friends, some of whom were not as motivated in school as I was. How far would they have made it? Would any of us have continued on to college? Hannah admires my scholarly accomplishments and expresses amazement at my hopes for the future. I don't think she sees that my position in life was formed by circumstance and chance.

A system has been propping me up all my life, the same system that oppresses other people in my own country and all over the world. The people who have money are able to help their children acquire the education, connections, and skills they need to make money themselves. If I had been born into a poor family in the U.S., most likely my life would not have led me to where I am now.

The system also includes the belief that wealth equals a successful life and that achievement in school can lead to wealth. While family is important, individual achievement is the more celebrated part of the mainstream U.S. cultural system. Although women are usually expected to sacrifice their individual pursuits for their families, at least they are allowed individual pursuits in the first place. They also have greater economic opportunity than women in Zimbabwe, simply because the U.S. economy can absorb more people. My research on baby dumping is teaching me how the different cultural systems in the U.S. and Zimbabwe affect women. I see that there is no end to what I have yet to learn.

Each document I read becomes another small piece of the puzzle for which I must find a place. I do not read constantly. Instead I spend time reflecting, and recalling information I learned previously. As I read through documents on education, I remember my interview with the Senior Mistress of Mount Pleasant School, Mrs. Nyangoni. The law states that a girl must leave school immediately upon becoming pregnant, she told me. The girl cannot return to school within the same year she gives birth. Most never return. According to Mrs. Nyangoni, once schoolgirls become pregnant, "there's nothing for them, it's a dead end. Most of them turn into prostitutes."

The policy of forcing pregnant girls to leave school implies that a girl's primary role is that of a potential mother and not a student. Few people seem to be searching for alternatives, such as creating a day-care center for children of students.

Prevention efforts through sex education and an explanation of birth control may be a long way off for Zimbabwean schoolchildren. Because of the attitude that girls' educational and employment opportunities are not as important as boys', girls are not given a fair chance to create a different future.

As I think about my perspective, I realize that my idea of what is "fair" for girls is from my own bias. Neither my ideas nor theirs are inherently the "right" ones to have. Yet I feel frustrated for the girls who might want to pursue an education but are thwarted by social, cultural, and economic pressures, and I believe other Zimbabwean women, like Hannah, share my feelings. I also realize that this situation for girls is not solely a Zimbabwean phenomenon. It occurs everywhere, including in the United States.

The most exciting part of my research is having my eyes opened to something I had never before considered. Mrs. Nyangoni did that for me when she explained that some of the schoolgirls' pregnancies stem from economic pressures on their families. She said, "In the general picture, the mother is not there. She is on communal lands while the daughter lives with her father or uncle in town." The father or uncle tries to find employment in town while the daughter attends school. "You get some uncles who bring lovers for a girl to supplement his income. The girls have no protection." If the girl becomes pregnant as a result of being prostituted, she must leave school, and she loses almost all potential for economic security. In being forced to strengthen her uncle's financial position, she loses much hope for her own future.

Because females' lives everywhere have always been sacrificed, literally or figuratively, for the benefit of males, I am not surprised that it happens here. However, when a man sees no opportunity for financial stability aside from selling his niece's body, sexism is not the only problem. I was reminded of this complexity last night when, after having dinner with the Mandazas, I entered into a rare conversation with Kenneth. I usually don't feel inclined to talk with him because I am upset at how hard he makes Hannah's life.

We began talking about employment opportunities. I was shocked when he said that if he were an employer, he would hire a white man over a black man. I asked if he thought a white man could do a better job than he could, and he said, "Yes." I asked if he based his opinion on the idea that whites may have had more education or experience in the workforce, and he just shrugged his shoulders. He seemed certain that whites could do a better job.

I found myself, a white person, arguing against a black person's conviction that whites are more capable workers than blacks. I asked him why he thought so poorly of himself and his race. "It's the colonial mentality," he said. Twelve years of independence from white rule does not erase the psychology of a history of oppression.

The colonial mentality destroys self-esteem in both men and women, and leads to financial instability. Add sexism, and the combination is devastating to women and girls all over Zimbabwe. Factors that lead one man to pay another for the experience of raping a schoolgirl are deeply rooted in history and culture. The whole situation caused by world systems and cultures frustrates and angers me. But most of all, I feel intense anguish and despair for the girls who bear the brunt of the worlds' problems.

I did not begin to grasp the economic significance of a pregnancy for an unmarried woman in Zimbabwe until today. It becomes clearer as I read a UNICEF study on Zimbabwe that explains how "access to employment [for] women [is] influenced by their socio-economic status, educational level and race." A single pregnant woman seeking employment is likely to be of a low socioeconomic status and possibly without much education. Her situation negatively affects her prospects of finding a job.

Furthermore, in *Women in Zimbabwe*, Elinor Batezat and Margaret Mwalo maintain that despite progressive anti-sex-discrimination measures such as maternity leave regulations and the 1981 Equal Pay for Equal Work regulations, "women's participation in formal employment has not significantly increased since 1981." A Zimbabwean woman who becomes pregnant while employed may even risk losing her job. Without hope for financial viability, a woman may see no way of raising her child and have no place to turn.

Norma Hall's University of Zimbabwe dissertation further indicates the impact of employment on infanticide. She discusses a 1984 study of thirty-five women in jail for infanticide. The study found that 71 percent of these women had been unemployed at the time of the offense. I imagine that employed women were earning very little as housekeepers or by selling tomatoes in the market. If a woman has difficulty obtaining employment or earning enough money and reaches a level of financial and emotional desperation, she may dump her baby. If she does so, she might be able to return to her family or at least have a better chance of finding employment in the future.

As I walk home through the crowds of people on the hot Harare sidewalks, I imagine the typical woman in a baby-dumping case. I see the young woman walking, as I am, through Harare and trying to find some hope, some help for herself and her baby. She sees, as I do, the woman with two young boys who sits on the sidewalk every day begging for money. She sees that the woman and her children are hungry and that people do not look at them as they pass by.

As I contemplate the young pregnant woman I have been learning about, I pass a group of men staring at me while smoking by the side of a building. I ask myself, "What influenced this woman's decision to have sex, and unprotected sex, in the first place?" I have gathered from several sources that partly because sex education in inaccessible, many young women are coerced into having not only sex, but unprotected sex. Sharon explained to me that frequently an inexperienced schoolgirl will hear a classmate, a teacher, or even a stranger tell her he loves her. This man may pursue her incessantly until she gives in.

There is also a character commonly referred to as the "sugar daddy," a somewhat wealthy older man who showers a young girl with gifts and expects sex in return. He may prey on her outside the school building by offering her a ride home in his car and lunch along the way. She may be encouraged by friends to accept his offers because he can give her luxurious gifts. Perhaps if girls felt hopeful that they could one day obtain luxuries for themselves, they would not be as likely to succumb to a sugar daddy.

Girls are not given guidance that offers perspectives on the men who pursue them or on the decisions they face. Instead they are left to make decisions they do not fully understand, and without information and support for their autonomy and well-being. They make choices under pressure from seemingly powerful males in a male-dominated society. One of these girls eventually becomes pregnant with a baby she does not want and cannot support. Having been abandoned by her community long ago, she cannot turn to this community for help. Finally she finds herself considering abandoning her own child.

Girls and women cannot always choose whether to become sexually involved with a man. They are blamed for being rape victims and for causing unwanted pregnancies, and society absolves men of responsibility. When I consider my question, "What influences a girl or woman to have sex in the first place," I find myself overwhelmed by the complexity of the answer.

A feeling of desperation washes over me as I uncover each new reason behind baby dumping, and it comes from the knowledge that these girls and women are trapped by social, cultural, and economic systems that in combination seem perfectly orchestrated to oppress females. They are held prisoner as surely as if they were imprisoned by stone walls without windows. While I don't believe that the girls are inevitable victims of society, I wonder how girls and women can break free of a perfect trap?

In reality, the trap only looks perfect. As women see how it is constructed and how they play a part in constructing it, they can begin to dismantle it and prevent other traps from being built. The word is spreading; women are becoming more aware of themselves and the illogic of their entrapment.

Even though it sometimes seems that men, long ago, mapped out a plan to oppress women, I don't really believe that happened. Both sexes, generally unaware and unquestioning, have contributed to the system. Because the system has benefited men, however, they tend to resist and suppress women's efforts to challenge the status quo. Therefore it is up to the women to break down the walls that surround them. As the picture of a solution takes form, my sense of desperation begins to subside. I am filled instead with determination as I imagine the enormous, bottled-up strength that the women inside the walls are only beginning to unleash.

After several days of success in locating the material I was looking for, I was unprepared for this morning. Once again, I find myself up against a brick wall. I tracked down University of Zimbabwe Professor Sarah Singende-Harris, who has completed the most extensive study of infanticide in Zimbabwe so far. She said she would like to talk with me about her study, but it has not been published yet. Child Survival (a nongovernmental organization) has the copyright, and she will not give me any information until Child Survival gives her permission. She told me where the Child Survival office is located and suggested I go there and ask for permission.

I arrived at Child Survival after some difficulty finding the right bus. I asked the woman in charge of copyrights for permission. She listened calmly to my request and then launched into an excited monologue about how Sarah wants more money, but Child Survival does not have that much money and if she releases the report to me then it will mean she's given in to Sarah's demands. She said that if I tell Sarah that Child Survival will not pay her more money and have Sarah call Child Survival to approve the deal, then she'll show me the report. Fed up with being caught in the middle of bureaucracy and other people's personal issues, I left the office. I called Sarah to tell her what the woman said and I gave her my phone number. I don't expect to hear from her, and in some ways I am relieved.

I have some time before lunch, so I start looking for the Government Publications Office that Sharon told me about. For once I do not have difficulty locating a place in Harare I've never visited before. However, finding the information I want is another story. I must wait for a librarian to help me locate some economic data. No one knows if or when he will arrive, but I want to be here in case that moment comes. Just as I begin to lose hope, the librarian shows up. He excavates a mine of books behind the counter and finds me an economics report from 1985. He tells me that these are the office's most recent economic data.

I sit down at a small desk to pore over the report. The librarian brings me what appears to be a reliable Demographic and Health Survey from 1986. What I find most interesting about these statistics is that they are compiled in a vacuum. Northern European countries gave grants for studies in certain years, such as from 1986-1990, but not before or since. So while I have statistics on one period, I cannot compare them with those from any other period. I do not know if other statistical records exist, and neither does the librarian for the Government Publications Office. The data still may be useful, so I spend a couple hours copying them down in my notebook. This is one of those times when I would happily pay five cents for a photocopy, were that a possibility.

I arrive at the Department of Social Services with a chip on my shoulder. This is a branch of the Police Department where I had the bad experience with the Officer Commanding Central. When I ask Mrs. Chinaka if she will talk to me for a moment about baby dumping, she asks me for a letter from my government. I tell her that I do not have one, that all I need to know is the role of the Department in treating destitute women and children. She says she cannot tell me anything without a letter of permission. The fact is, the information I am seeking from her is not crucial to my paper. I tell her: "I don't have time to obtain permission and this information is not crucial to me so I won't try. I do want to tell you that I think this policy is working against the interests of the Social Services Department. I know that this Department refers women to ABC, and I want my project to help ABC."

I am about to turn and leave when I notice Mrs. Chinaka pause. Without even trying, I think I have somehow persuaded her to reconsider.

"Do you have a letter from your school?" she asks.

I hand her two general letters from my directors, and she leads me into her office. "What do you want to know?" she asks. I have finally found a crack in the bureaucratic wall. As I ask her my basic questions, she begins to open up without much encouragement. She sits back in her chair and tells me: "Indirectly, the parents encourage the expectant mother to abandon the baby. They'll say to her, 'Take the child to its father.'" But the father usually rejects her. She says that in addition to baby dumping, the police are "seeing a lot of suicide, as well."

I wonder how much influence Mrs. Chinaka has on the Harare Social Services system. She seems aware of the complexities of the baby-dumping problem and regularly refers women to ABC and Shelter Trust. However, the government neither gives financial assistance to these two overworked, under-financed organizations that it appears to rely on, nor does it offer any alternatives to their services. I imagine how much more effective the Abandoned Babies' Committee and Shelter Trust could be if the Department of Social Services offered them financial assistance rather than only referrals.

I have fifty questions for my interviews at the day center today. I have reminded Amai Mamutse every day this week that I would come with her today, and she is actually here in the office where I wait. I glance toward the door as two young women come in. They are selling perfume, earrings and cosmetics. The more aggressive of the two used to stay at the Shelter Trust home. Now she tries to support herself and her child by going to Johannesburg to buy goods and then sell them here.

I interview five young women who tell me the same story: social and economic pressure and hopelessness. They are all at the Day Center because someone knew they needed help and sent them to see Amai Mamutse. Amai recognized that these women were at risk of the kind of desperation that can lead a woman to abandon her baby. The day center is a large room containing benches and some tables. Of the two tables at the front of the room, one holds three sewing machines and some fabric. The other displays finished products for sale, including school uniforms, clothespin bags, and a skirt. Next to the tables on a large rug are toys to occupy children and at the back of the room four more tables. Amai Mamutse explains that because the day is overcast and cooler than usual, fewer than the usual number of women have come. Only six women are present over the course of the day, some with their children. During the interviews, I sit in the back of the room in order to have privacy.

Because this is the first time I have met the women, I do not expect them to divulge their innermost thoughts and feelings. In addition to the lack of time developing trust, the language barrier limits the depth of our communication. These are not well-educated women, and their English skills are only slightly better than my Shona. And although they are willing to talk to me, they are uncomfortable discussing the personal journeys that led them to the day center.

They repeatedly stress their terrible, endless struggle to feed and clothe their children. They tell me they have been "chased away" or beaten by a boyfriend, a husband, or family. Some of the women talk hopefully of their plans to sell tomatoes or the garments they have sewn. But the women who have been coming here longer are far less hopeful. While each woman receives a share of the profits from day center sales, Elizabeth tells me she usually receives "less than ten dollars a month."

Even after having had babies, the women are unaware of birth control methods. Most do not know what adoption is. Although they might benefit from Maintenance law, none of them can tell me what the law means or how it could help them. Amai Mamutse tries to make this information available to the women, but she does not have time to explain everything.

As they speak, they bring home the reality of what I am studying. I have spent time searching for statistics on the number of baby-dumping cases, and I have been frustrated by not being able to find accurate numbers. The women remind me that the numbers do not matter. Whether there are fifty cases or five hundred, the issues need to be addressed. The suffering is real.

The women avoid talking about baby dumping even though,

according to Amai Mamutse, none of them did it. Baby dumping is a sensitive issue. The act itself, the circumstances that lead to it, and the women involved all are judged harshly. Unfortunately, if those who are most affected by the issue do not discuss it, others can ignore it.

I sit with each woman and listen to her describe the factors that make her an outcast in society. As each one speaks, my desire is to communicate my respect for her struggle to survive in the face of so many odds. I wish the women did not feel ashamed or so much more responsible than the rest of the community. I believe that their condition should not reflect on them to the exclusion of the world around them.

Amai Mamutse invites me to her house after we finish at the day center. On the way there in the E.T., she tells me that she has eight children who are in school. I do not know how she manages to support them. She also is one of eight children. Three of her siblings are "deaf and dumb," she says. As a result of having grown accustomed to signing, she sometimes has difficulty verbalizing her thoughts.

As the E.T. careens along the road, I find myself glancing at Amai from time to time, just to make sure she is real. There is a powerful calm in her that intrigued me during our first interview. The more I learn about her life and work, the more her calm strength fascinates and inspires me.

Amai Mamutse was awake before 6:00 a.m. this morning to go to the hospital to visit a sick single mother. She says she has to go because the woman has no family. For Amai there is no question whether or not the woman needed *someone* to visit her. The reason she does such things as visit a sick woman she barely knows in the hospital is that she sees all people as "family." In her earnest and matter-of-fact manner, she explains that because her own family has suffered, she understands and cares about the suffering of others.

After leaving the hospital, Amai went to the day center to help destitute women find some hope for their future. When she left the center, a woman with an infant was waiting for her outside. Not having eaten and having nowhere to live, they had been searching for Amai Mamutse. There is little she can do. Amai Mamutse has no money and she frequently uses her own money to help others. She pays for her own transportation wherever she goes on behalf of ABC, which is a significant expense.

The two of them spoke in Shona, and after the woman left, I asked Amai what will happen to her. She said she hopes there will be room for her at a shelter or that she can find a friend or relative to stay with until she can earn some money.

Amai lives in a high-density area. The dirt roads teem with children, and many of the homes look as though a strong wind would push them over. Her second-grade daughter is outside selling Freeze-its when we arrive. I did not expect lunch, but Amai serves me a large helping of sadza and potatoes. She says one of her "deaf and dumb" sisters and the sister's baby live with her. The sister was chased away by her husband's family after his recent death, leaving her without even a change of clothes. Since theirs was a marriage under customary law only, it is unlikely that the civil courts will grant her inheritance money.

Amai Mamutse's father had tried hard to persuade her sister to have a registered civil marriage, but the husband always refused. Now she is destitute. Although Amai says that "it's a burden" having the two extra people in the house, she does not say it with bitterness or desperation. I do not know how she manages to remain calm and forward-looking with all the challenges before her. Something about her tells me that she can imagine no other way to be.

In the afternoon we return to the ABC office where she gives me more literature to read while she works. She says she does not understand why many African organizations are possessive about their information. She asks, "How can we learn if we don't work with other people?" That is why she is so generous with me.

This evening, she has a meeting with HIV-positive mothers. "For charity," she is doing a study of forty HIV mothers. So far she has interviewed six. I do not know where she finds the time. She says that HIV is an increasing cause of baby dumping, and she has already seen five such cases. Pregnant women who know they are infected or who have developed AIDS are even more hopeless and desperate than healthy women with unwanted pregnancies. As we talk, it becomes clear to me that Amai Mamutse never stops working. She cares about the fact that so many women need her help.

Whenever I leave Amai Mamutse, I feel energized and inspired by her dedication and hard work. But when I return to my notebooks full of information about the roots of baby dumping and the condition of women in Zimbabwe, my positive outlook falters. Amai Mamutse seems so alone in her struggle.

The problems behind baby dumping have grown important to me. I accept the fact that in my limited time I cannot begin to have an impact. At the same time I feel that I will be walking away from a fire burning out of control. Sometimes I feel selfish for planning to leave and return to my comfortable college life. Clearly there is an immediate need for help. I have no way to support myself, but I feel the urge to stay and do the work that needs to be done.

College brought me here in the first place, and I believe that finishing school will allow me to take advantage of my position in life and make the greatest contribution. I do not know what role I can play in solving the problems of the world, but I don't think that staying here would be the most effective one. I am committed to doing my part and to finding out what that part should be. In the meantime, I need reassurance that somebody will help Amai Mamutse put out the fire.

My greatest hope focuses on the women's organizations I have encountered in Zimbabwe as well as from the individuals who are working to make changes for Zimbabwean women. I do trust that others here are slowly but surely chipping away at the obstacles to women's freedom. Each rock these people manage to pry out of the way is the beginning of a new and smoother path. When I return to Zimbabwe, I expect to see many footprints on these new paths.

I find a bench to sit on in Harare Gardens. The sun is blazing down on me and on the brittle, yellow lawn surrounding me. The glare compels me to close my eyes. In this hot darkness I find myself unable to stop thinking about the baby-dumping problem. Slowly as the large circle of issues takes over my mind, I move through it and name each jagged piece I see. I know there are many I cannot see and will not find during my remaining time in Zimbabwe.

I imagine the puzzle pieces forming a circle around women with unwanted pregnancies. The circle tightens with each additional piece. Women are less likely to be educated than are men. The Zimbabwean economy is struggling with drought and a controversial economic policy. When the economy falters and unemployment rises, opportunities for women become even more scarce because men are the first to be hired.

The women in the center of the circle need a way out through the tiny cracks between pieces of circumstance, policy, and practice. Unfortunately, they may not know about the Abandoned Babies' Committee or Shelter Trust, and are probably ignorant of the laws that might help them. Parents have chased them away; the babies' fathers are nowhere to be found. Guided by the image of this massive puzzle and the women caught within it, I leave Harare Gardens to complete my research.

# TANHATU
(SIX)

# ENDING

# I  Relating: Hannah II

**F**irst run over to the Abandoned Babies' Committee. Then dash over to WAG to get the name of the man who wrote that article I read last week. Why is this street so busy today? Maybe I should go to WAG first. "Perrin!" Did someone call my name? I stop and turn around and find myself looking at Hannah. Suddenly all thoughts of my schedule disappear. What is Hannah doing in the city? Before I even say hello, she begins explaining why she is here.

Behind her is Lisa, her neighbor who is related to the Mandazas by marriage. Lisa is twenty-one years old and pregnant with her first child. Hannah is accompanying her to the doctor because the baby is due this week. I am happy to see Hannah and surprised to run into her because she rarely leaves the house in Southerton. We quickly arrange for me to call her this week and for us to see each other on Saturday. Lisa tugs at Hannah's sleeve, indicating it is time for them to go.

As Hannah says good-bye to me, Lisa begins to cross the street. Hannah glances at her and then pauses long enough to miss the light. She cannot cross the street now.

"Hannah, how are you doing?" She looks as if she wants to talk to me.

"Oh, I am not happy!" She is not looking at me.

"Why not? What is wrong?" These questions seem ridiculous, given the situation I know she is living in.

She answers listlessly, "I don't know. I'm thinking too much."

Knowing that she will have to join Lisa in a moment, I have no patience for her evasiveness. I want to know what is wrong. "Hannah! Tell me! What are you thinking about?"

"Oh, about life."

"What about life?"

"I'm confused."

A busy street corner with Lisa growing more impatient by the second is not the place for a heart-to-heart talk, but I am too concerned to let it go. I ask, "You're confused about what?"

She sighs, "My school. My education."

Hannah has not finished school yet, but she has not been enrolled for years. Something else must be going on.

"What else, Hannah?"

"It is not good to say, 'I need two dollars,' 'I want to go to town,' all the time. I don't do anything all day except stay in the house. It is not good."

"I know." I know. And I wish more than anything that your life were different. You deserve so much more than what you have. While I am glad she is opening up to me, her words are hard to hear.

She tells me, "I saw Sam on Saturday." Sam is her boyfriend.

"Did you tell him what you've been thinking about?"

"Yes."

"What did he say?" I am not sure if I want to hear the answer to this one.

"He was very busy. He had to go to some company."

At that moment, Lisa calls for her to come. Hannah looks at me with her large brown eyes, and then crosses the street. As she walks off with Lisa, I stand on the corner, still trying to digest Sam's response to her. It seems to me that if he wants to marry her, he should take an interest when she tells him about her serious thoughts about the future. I hope she doesn't marry him. I cannot wait to see her this weekend, when we can have a longer talk.

Hannah arrived at our meeting place for lunch an hour after we had planned. She said that Mr. Mandaza almost forbade her to come. I had called her on Wednesday to arrange to meet her today at noon. Mr. Mandaza was there when I called, and when we hung up she told him of our arrangements. Well, this morning Amai and Baba Mandaza came to the conclusion that she had lied about having plans with me and was really coming to see her boyfriend. They said she was lying to them and they would not allow her to come. They said she would get pregnant.

Truthfully, Hannah and I had been discussing meeting Sam in town because I have not yet met him. However, she did not lie about having plans with me. Upset by Amai and Baba's reaction, Hannah told them that she would call and tell me exactly why she could not come meet me. At that point, they agreed to let her go. Sometimes when she talks about her life at the Mandazas', I forget that she is twenty-seven years old. According to Shona custom, she will not be considered an adult until she is married and has children. She may never be considered an autonomous individual. Now that she is here, we decide to call Sam to see if he will have lunch with us. I do not feel that we are betraying the Mandazas because there is no chance that she will become pregnant over lunch with the two of us. He agrees to meet us, and while we wait, I buy her a chocolate milkshake. She sips it very slowly as we talk. I would like to continue the conversation we started on the street corner on Monday, but I don't want to be interrupted by Sam.

We go to one of the few restaurants in the area that serve "western" foods like sandwiches and chocolate milkshakes. When Sam arrives, we order our food. It takes Hannah a while to decide on something. A lot of the items on the menu may not be familiar to her. Sam appears nice enough, but I cannot help analyzing his every word and gesture.

Over lunch, he asks me many questions about U.S. politics and compares the U.S. with Zimbabwe. I bring up the issue of women in politics because I am interested in his reaction. "Most Zimbabwean women don't like politics," he says. My ears perk up; Hannah and I have had several conversations on the subject. I ask him why that is, and he responds, "Zimbabwean politics don't benefit women." His answer impresses me, although I cannot discern whether or not it bothers him that Zimbabwean politics do not benefit women.

I look at Hannah because I am interested in her response to his comments. She looks at the floor with her head tilted to one side, her hands in her lap, almost as if she were not paying attention, though I am sure she is. "Hannah, what do you think?" She barely answers me.

I have never seen her in this state. It does not even look as if she is thinking. I know she tends to be quiet with people, but I had assumed that she would feel comfortable enough around Sam to talk; after all, she expects to marry him. Is she "playing dumb?" Suddenly it occurs to me that maybe she is flirting. Sharon mentioned to me that girls learn to act coquettish and dumb around boys in order to be attractive to them. I have seen the same kind of behavior in the U.S., but never to this extreme.

I cannot believe that Hannah is behaving in this way. I am sure she has a lot to say on the issue of women and politics, yet she refuses to speak. The idea that her boyfriend believes she has no thoughts on such issues, or that he finds such behavior attractive, appalls me. Sam and I continue talking throughout lunch, Hannah does not say a word. I cannot shake a sense of disappointment and sadness.

After lunch Sam leaves, and Hannah and I begin to walk down the street. I had planned to come with her to Southerton after lunch to say hello to Amai and Baba Mandaza. When she tells me that no one will be home, I write them a note, partly to prove to them that Hannah really was planning to meet me today. Hannah and I decide to walk away from the center of town so that we can continue our talk.

I tell her about my research on baby dumping. I am almost finished gathering information and it is time for me to start writing the paper. She asks me what I have learned, so I describe my conclusions. She nods her head as I speak, occasionally adding a point of her own. The intent way in which she listens leads me to explain practically my entire project.

When I finish, I ask her what she thinks. I want to know if what I have said sounds valid to her. She slows down and with her soft voice full of conviction, she says, "You speak the truth.

What you say is true." We then walk quietly until we are outside the city.

In many ways, the lessons I've learned from Hannah have become the framework for my understanding of Zimbabwe. My experiences and perspectives have gathered within that frame. Her existence has motivated me even when the great effort it takes to participate fully in Zimbabwe overwhelms me. A couple of times I had what I thought of as paralysis. Lying on my bed, feeling much too hot but unable to move, I would not want to stand up and enter the world around me.

At those times, I felt like a fallen statue, so heavy and lifeless. I couldn't help it. I broke out of my paralysis by sheer will and by believing that the rewards of my effort would be worth the risk of cracking the statue. I would stand up and little by little move myself back into the world.

When I lived in the Mandazas' house, Hannah was always there when I emerged. She would be cleaning or preparing a meal. Seeing her living her life always shook me free of the fallen statue. Hannah has never had the luxury of choosing whether to stand up or stay in bed, and the kind of tired she feels is not the stone statue kind. Hers is being the flame of a candle cowering in an incessant wind that could extinguish her.

I learn from Hannah all the time. We have the kind of friendship in which many of our most important conversations happen in a meeting of our eyes rather than with words. I have never felt more in touch with humanity than when Hannah and I connect across our vastly different backgrounds. At those times, it feels as if I am the first person ever to discover human beings. It feels as if I understand that there is only one human being. Hannah's oppression is my oppression; I believe that it is only by chance that I am not she, and she is not I.

Hannah is always shaping my perspective. When I returned from my first visit in Wachikwa and told her how special I thought the village was, she rolled her eyes and told me she would hate rural life. "It is too much work," she said. She was right, and she reminds me all the time of the reality of women born and raised in Zimbabwe versus my reality as a visitor. Often in a conversation about the right of women to be treated as men's equals, Hannah, without saying a word, would leave to prepare food for the boys. In such moments I understood the depth of sexist oppression.

Her life has informed me that while there must be policies to support women's equality, there also needs to be a waterfall of attention to smooth the cultural obstacles. I thought about that need when I saw Victoria Falls. I remember wishing for something exactly that powerful and thunderous to clear the path in Hannah's life.

Hannah is not hopeless. She often mentions her desire for an education, and I believe she may find a way to finish school. But she has little ambition compared to what my imagination conjures up. I have dreamt her into a school where some teacher notices her special brightness and guides her toward a satisfying, fulfilling future. She has no reason for ambition. Why would she think she could find a scholarship? What in her life leads her to feel that only the sky is the limit?

I have told her my dreams, and she smiles. I think she likes my dreams the way children like a good fairy tale. Her smile reminds me over and over again of the gap between what one wants and what one believes it possible to have. In my own life, I have always felt that the gap could be made quite small. She has shown me how wide and deep it can be. She has shown me how real it is. In many ways, she has been my metronome here, keeping me focused in time and space.

My knowing Hannah has also influenced my baby dumping project. I have committed myself to that project as if my life depends on finding out all the reasons why baby dumping occurs and how to stop it. Actually, I think I work on that project as if Hannah's life depends on it. It helps me understand the social, cultural, and economic systems that have shaped her existence. The moment I told Hannah my conclusions and she said, "What you say is true," I felt as if I had achieved some kind of justice by doing what I could to understand her position in this web of life.

A taxi screeches around the corner just before we step off the curb to cross the street. When we safely reach the other side, I look at Hannah.

"Hannah, I want to talk to you more about your future."

"Oh, I don't want to talk about this."

"Are you still thinking about school?"

"Yes. I am confused."

"About what?"

"Oh, I don't want to talk about this. I have no money for school."

"How much does it cost?"

"We talk about something else."

As she changes the subject, I am reminded of why I did not want to end our conversation on the street corner the other day. It is so rare for Hannah to discuss her life with me. She usually does not want to talk about possibilities for her future or even what she thinks about her present. For some reason, that day she was willing.

I hope that even though she is averse to talking about it, she will think about it. I can tell that she is not in the mood to discuss Sam either, so we talk about Wachikwa, rural life, and politics. We cover some of the same political issues that Sam brought up at lunch.

By the time Hannah needs to return to Southerton, we have conversed about everything except the important issues in her life. While that exasperates me, I rejoice in seeing her again. I do not want her to leave, because I enjoy being with her. However, I too will be leaving soon. In less than three weeks, I will leave Zimbabwe. Hannah tells me that she will come to the airport to say goodbye to me.

As we discuss my leaving, we become sad, and she tells me that I should not forget her. "I could not forget you," I say. "I know," she smiles. As she boards the bus, I watch her settle into a window seat wearing a quiet expression on her face. I respect her decisions concerning when to discuss her life with me. She does not have many opportunities to make choices, so I accept the ones she does make. I walk away from the bus feeling lucky to know Hannah Moyo.

## II Parting: Kyanderes

I am so late. I am so late, and Amai Mamutse might leave before I arrive at ABC. If I do not see her today, I will not be able to start this section of my paper for another two days. I slam the door of the room I have been sharing with another student in a cheap hotel in Harare, and run down the stairs. This has been a convenient place to stay while I conduct my research. Right now, however, I wish it were much closer to ABC. I fly past the second floor, hoping that the man who always stands there and tries to reel me into a conversation isn't home. I make it safely past his floor.

I rush through the small entrance-room of the hotel. Two people stand by the door staring at me. I aim for the door, and glance at my watch. Suddenly it dawns on me that the person blocking my way, right in front of the door, looks familiar. So does the person next to her. I stop dead in my tracks, "Amai! Baba! What are you doing here?!" My Amai and Baba from Wachikwa are standing right in front of me. They are dressed up in city clothes and they have come to visit me, remembering that in less than two weeks I will leave the country.

They seem as overwhelmed as I am that they happen to be here and they explain in fragmented sentences that they came because I will leave soon. They are so happy that they did not miss me. So am I. We walk outside the entrance, and I have to keep looking at them to make sure they are really here. I have never seen them in a city environment. I feel self-conscious in my pants. Although pants are not considered "inappropriate" in the city, no women in rural areas like Wachikwa wear them. I certainly wore only long skirts there. I feel like a child caught sneaking around behind my parents' backs. I guess they'll have to get used to seeing me in the city environment, as well. I am truly shocked that they are here. I never expected them actually to come.

As we stand outside, making small talk and staring at each other, my Amai reaches into her purse. I didn't even know she owned a purse. No one has to carry a purse in Wachikwa. I wonder what she has in it. She pulls out a plastic bag and takes out a beautiful, creamy lace doily. She drapes it over my outstretched arms and tells me, "This is for your Amai ku U.S.A." She crocheted this for my mother. "Amai, tatenda. This is so beautiful. My Amai ku U.S.A. will love it. If you would like, I will send you a picture of her with this." I don't know how to thank her for this gift.

There is something beautiful inside of Amai Kyandere that compels her to make beautiful things, and to give them in a beautiful way. She was thinking about and caring about and wanting to give something to my mother. The only response I can think of is to clap my hands in the formal way as I say, "Tatenda chaizvo, Amai. And tatenda chaizvo Amai and Baba Kyandere for coming here to Harare to say goodbye to me."

By this time we are smiling. I am so excited that they have come and that I can see them one more time. "Tonderai, we only stay for a short time," Baba says to me with a grave look. "That's OK, Baba. I am glad you came." Amai explains, "We go to see Baba's brothers. We cannot pay the bus to come to Harare many times. We are here, so we must see Baba's brothers today." I say, "I understand."

We walk to African National Unity Square and pass the fountain as the breeze sends a mist over us. There are no free benches, so we choose a space on the grass to sit. Once again, my Amai reaches into her purse. Again I am curious about what she has in there. Out of it she pulls her familiar faded-pink, Java-print wrap. She wears this as a skirt almost daily in Wachikwa. When she is not wearing it, she and others use it to sit on outside. Sitting beside Amai and Baba on the wrap with the pictures of animals running across it, I can only smile. The city clothes and the traffic noise don't change anything.

I tell Amai and Baba that I am almost finished with school. My project is due next week. They smile and tell me they are happy for me. I have been immersed in the issue of baby dumping, but I know it would be inappropriate to dwell on it with Amai and Baba. There may be a way to approach it that would not be insensitive to their experience, but I can't take the risk of bringing up painful thoughts for them. It takes me a moment to adjust my train of thought.

I ask them about Wachikwa, Baba's cows, and the women from the women's club. They both laugh hard when I ask if the vegetables have been growing in a wavy line as a result of my attempt to plow. They exclaim that the vegetables are growing very well. I am sure they fixed my rows after I left, but they would never tell me that. I notice that when I talk about the city and my activities here, I talk much faster than when we talk about Wachikwa.

A woman walks by and does not look at us, but Amai quietly stares at her as she passes. In Wachikwa, Amai taught me to greet anyone who crosses my line of vision. Since Wachikwa is flat, that sometimes meant a person walking quite far away. We always called out a greeting, and the person always responded. Of course the city is different, but it feels strange to watch Amai in a new context. I feel that the woman who passed us should have greeted her.

Something about my meeting with Amai and Baba feels like a foreshadowing of what I will experience when I return to the United States. I imagine simultaneously having a conversation with someone and thinking only of Zimbabwe. As with Amai and Baba and the baby-dumping issue, I may not know how to express my thoughts in a way that will make me understood. Maybe there will be a way to communicate about my experience, but will I know how, or when to try?

I also imagine myself in Amai and Baba's position upon my return to the U.S. As the Kyanderes sit in a park in Harare, the people who pass them do not know or care that Amai and Baba woke up this morning in a small, quiet village. The identities that Amai and Baba have in Wachikwa are irrelevant here. Once they leave the village, these identities only matter inside of them. The true value of the identities lies in how they help Amai and Baba define who they truly are and what is important to them.

I have an identity here in Zimbabwe. It is the result of the life I have lived and the people I have known and who have known me in Harare and in Wachikwa. While I remain in Zimbabwe, this identity develops along with each relationship or new experience. When I leave Zimbabwe, this identity will remain inside the people I have known and it will remain inside me. As I enter the United States, the true value of my identity here will be its power to help me define inside myself who I am and what is important to me. As the breeze envelops me in the cool fountain mist, I look at Amai and Baba. Identities do not change with city clothes or the presence of strangers. It only looks that way. I picture Wachikwa and ask if everything there looks the same. "Oh, yes. Wachikwa is the same." It is nice to spend a moment in an image that doesn't change. Through the noon hour, Amai, Baba and I chat about nothing important. A vague thought of my "urgent" need to go to ABC today gently disappears from my mind. The conversation flows back and forth, and I do not notice the people walking by or even the light that shifts into afternoon.

When Baba asks me what time it is, I realize that our visit has come to an end. It is time for Baba and Amai to visit with Baba's brother. As we walk toward the bus stop, I look for a meat shop. I was never able to bring meat to Baba because it would have spoiled during the long, hot trip to Wachikwa. Night after night, he told Amai and me that he missed meat more than anything. Meat is expensive, made even more so by the number of cattle killed as a result of the drought. If I give meat to him now, they can eat it at his brother's house before heading back to Wachikwa. I finally spot a butcher and tell Amai and Baba to wait. When I present Baba with his meat, his smile is filled with gratitude and anticipation of the meal to come. I always felt that what Baba missed the most about meat was not the taste but the sense it gave him of having something special, something coveted.

I wish I had a gift for Amai, but all I have is a pen from my backpack. She is the village secretary, so I know she will use it. I tell her to write me a letter with it. She asks me to promise to send her photos of me and my mother upon my return to the U.S. I promise. I know that the best gift I could give her is to send photos as soon as I return. Then she will know I remember her. It is time for them to leave. As they step onto the bus, I am smiling. I smile at Baba and his proud posture, his quiet, honest nature. I smile at Amai and her fierce strength, the beauty inside her. They sit next to each other, and in their city clothes no one would know they do not come from here. They smile back at me, their eyes shining. The bus pulls away from the curb.

# III  Resolving: Baby Dumping — Concluding the Project

I just went to an afternoon showing of the movie *Sarafina*. The theater was full, and I sat near the front. When I looked behind me, I saw only three or four other white faces. The film depicts the violent struggle in South Africa. At its most violent, moments when I felt most disturbed by the cruelty and injustice of the apartheid system, the rest of the audience laughed uproariously. That happened several times throughout the movie.

The violence was based on the reality of life in South Africa and mirrors situations Zimbabweans encountered during their own liberation struggle not long ago. After the movie, I asked the man next to me why he had laughed so much during the violent scenes. He shrugged his shoulders and said, "This is nothing." The silver screen violence is nothing compared to what this audience has experienced. That thought does not strike me as something to laugh about.

Now walking home along the bright sidewalk, I notice a man walking beside me, looking at me curiously. "How do you know our national anthem," he asks. Suddenly, I realize that I have been humming the anthem as I walked. I think a song in *Sarafina* reminded me of it. I laugh and explain that I am a student here, and we learned the anthem in Shona class. He smiles, "My name is Paul, what is yours?"

Paul and I continue walking, and he asks me other questions about what I am doing in Zimbabwe. When I explain my baby-dumping project, he becomes animated and wants to know what I have learned. This is the first time I have had to summarize my project for someone, and I have no idea where to start. I begin by asking him why he thinks a woman would dump her baby.

"I don't know. Maybe these women are unhappy because they do not want a baby. But it is very bad to kill the baby."

Now I know where to start. I want him to understand why the woman is unhappy and to see that her desire for the baby is not necessarily the central issue. As I launch into the profile of the typical woman who dumps her baby, we walk into the Terreskane bar and take a seat outside. This may be a long conversation.

Paul listens to me intently and nods his head as I try to synthesize all the information I have gathered into a coherent explanation. I wonder why he finds the issue fascinating. He tells me that he is interested in his culture, and this issue reflects his culture. I learn that he is a student of Military History at the University of Zimbabwe and is intrigued by the idea of military, governmental, economic, social, and cultural systems that profoundly affect individual lives. In the baby-dumping issue, he sees the systems that weave a web around the pregnant women.

The metal chairs at Terreskane are becoming uncomfortable, and Paul invites me to have tea at his cousin's apartment down the street. He would like his cousin, also a UZ student, to meet me. His cousin is not home, but Paul prepares tea for me anyway. The one-bedroom apartment is well-kept, with a television, telephone, two couches, and some plants. The small windows let in little light, so we turn on a lamp and relax with our tea.

When I tell Paul that I will be leaving Zimbabwe in a couple of weeks, he says to me very seriously, "You must come back soon." I look at him, not understanding the urgency in his voice. He says Zimbabwe needs more people to address issues like baby dumping. "We need your help," he tells me.

I have known for the whole time of researching this project that it is important. However, hearing him say that my help is needed makes my heart sink because I am not staying on, and I don't know how to help. "I will come back, and I will try to help; I just need to figure out how," I respond. He is unaware of ABC and the other women's organizations that work toward solving these issues. I describe the organizations to Paul so that he realizes I am not the only one who is thinking about the baby dumping problem. Informing him helps to reassure him and relax me.

I finally leave the apartment after two cups of tea and return home as the sky begins to darken. I had given myself a day off, but tomorrow I must begin the writing process. I have one week in which to write a paper that is supposed to be a minimum of forty pages, and I am concerned that I will not have enough information to fill them. No matter how much time I spend in researching, I still have so many unanswered questions.

Back in my room, I realize that talking with Paul has energized me and helped me focus the project. I pull out my notes and try to envision how I should begin. The outline seems easy; I will have a section for each of the different pressures on women that lead to baby dumping. I put "government and law" first. I write out the whole outline before I realize that the "government and law" section cannot go first. Zimbabweans do not orient themselves around laws and government in the way that people in the U.S. do. Zimbabweans are oriented most significantly around cultural systems that are separate from "government and law." I might learn as much from writing this paper as I have from researching it.

It is two in the morning and I am surrounded by stacks, mountains of grey index cards piled on the yellow bedspread. On each card is a piece of information, quote, or idea I want to include in the paper. I transferred my notes and interview reports onto these hundreds of cards because it was the only way I could think of to organize my paper. Since I do not have a computer, advance planning is necessary.

Each of the stacks around me is made up of cards whose subjects relate to each other; each stack comprises a block of reasons why baby dumping occurs. I tower over all of these reasons. I can arrange them and I can topple them with a swipe of my hand. In my paper, I want to arrange these reasons, present these stacks of information in a way that might help Zimbabweans knock them down.

After two days of writing, transforming each note jotted down on an index card into a complete thought, I rest. I lie on a bench in Harare Gardens listening to the breeze move through grass and leaves around me. The sun bakes my skin, but after crouching over my notebook in my room for two days, I like it. I didn't want to stop writing, but I had to because my hand hurt and I figured my brain was next. Yet I cannot stop thinking about my project.

I have used only half of my note cards, but already I have filled around fifty pages. I write for hours without breaks because it fascinates me how each piece of information links to another. Writing is allowing me to discover those links. I am curious to see where this chain takes me.

My writing will be finished in the next two or three days. Then my roommate and I will rent a computer for a couple of days in order to type our papers. I want to give Amai Mamutse a typed copy of my project, rather than a hand-written one. The other reports she has in her office are typed. The warm breeze that sweeps from my feet up to my head lulls me into relaxation. Still, I feel an energy waiting to pull me back to my project.

Page 87. I waited until I had typed the entire body of the paper into the computer before I could face writing a conclusion. The text is complete. I need to conclude this project. Flipping through my notecards, I check whether I have left out important points. I have not included all the cards in the paper, but I have said everything I want to say.

I am at the end of a chain of words describing the roots of the baby-dumping problem. The chain winds through Shona cultural views of women, men, family, sex, and children. It slips along beside the woman who dumps her baby and the legal system that she enters. The chain leads me through the doors of non-governmental organizations addressing women and their needs, and then behind the walls of the national family planning system. It stretches through the thirsty economy and the social pressures that claw at girls and women.

The chain wraps itself around women who, often without knowing the potential consequences, become sexually involved with men. If they become pregnant, they often have nowhere to turn. They are in an extremely vulnerable position, physically and emotionally. All their unmet needs for financial and emotional support, family planning information, and hope for self-reliance, added to the influence of sexual pressure and negative imagery, culminate in their decision to dump their babies.

I am reminded of a letter to the editor I read in the *Herald*. In his letter, D. Nhidza wrote, "It's true that 'it takes two to make a baby,' but it is equally false that it takes two to dump a baby." That pervasive attitude ignores the reasons behind baby dumping. In fact it takes many more than "two" people to make baby dumping occur. It takes a whole community of people unsupportive of and unresponsive to a woman's needs. That baby dumping can occur in a culture that values family and children points above all else to a missing link between what is valued and what is protected.

I find myself now looking beyond the edge of a cliff, and here the chain ends. Just as there is land beyond this cliff that I cannot reach, there is no conclusion to my project. The missing link must be found, and the chain continue growing. Women and men here must add links to the chain to make a bridge that will carry them to the next landing. This is where I leave the chain to be picked up by someone else.

As I type the last words of my paper, I feel myself holding onto the chain. Perhaps a part of it is for me to take, to show others, and continue to build. I turn off the computer, close my notebook, and walk out of my room. Down the stairs, out the door and onto the sidewalk. The sky is overcast, and there are no cars driving by.

I walk under the trees blooming red and watch as a green leaf floats to the ground. I stop and pick up it up, feeling the waxy surface and smooth edges. Putting it in my pocket, I continue walking down the sidewalk. I don't know exactly where I am heading, but I know what I am taking with me.

# IV  Releasing: History of Oppression

My sandaled feet grip the earth as I walk up the hill through the brush and dirt. My skirt swishes around my ankles, and a sudden gust of wind pulls my hair tightly away from my face. The higher I climb up the hill, the more majestic the scene around me. Gentle valleys cradle brush in shades of yellow, green, and grey. The valleys meet the edges of rocky hillsides that hold trees and brush that rustle in the wind. The valleys and hills ripple out to the horizon. And in the distance where the edge of the land seems to touch the sky, the most tremendous cloud I have ever seen hangs suspended. It is the deepest gray, almost purple, and I can feel the energy that moves it toward where I stand.

I had heard of Cecil John Rhodes when I was in the United States. But I don't think I ever knew exactly what he had done. Perhaps I had learned that he was a British "explorer." Did I know that he had "explored" Africa? Did I know what he had done to Africa? In Zimbabwe, I have learned about Cecil Rhodes.

Rhodes started his domination of Africa in the Cape of Good Hope, what is now Cape Town, South Africa. In 1879, Rhodes became "Prime Minister" of the Cape of Good Hope. I wonder what "Prime Minister" meant to the indigenous people who already had their own leadership. Through the diamond riches of the area, Rhodes acquired wealth that gave him power. He used his power to persuade the British and others on the Cape to support his efforts to expand his power.

The Shona and Ndebele lived on the land that is now Zimbabwe, the land to the north of Rhodes's new domain. As Rhodes set his sights on that northern land, he initiated a century of brutal oppression. First he sent missionaries because he knew that the Ndebele king was friendly to them. King Lobengula was friendly to them because he welcomed the opportunity for the education they brought to the region. The king allowed them to build schools, but he never let them preach their religion. The group of missionaries Rhodes sent in

1888, however, had an agenda greater than Christianity. These missionaries interpreted the English documents for Lobengula as he signed away some control of his land. Of course, Lobengula did not yet know that Rhodes was like the serpent in the stories the missionaries told.

And Britain was feeding the serpent. The British granted Rhodes a charter that gave him the "right" to administer all lands north of the Limpopo River (between what is now South Africa and Zimbabwe). He could also govern as far east as the Portuguese land (Mozambique) and as far west as the Belgian territory (Zaire) and the Portuguese land (Angola). Rhodes had no northern boundary. He announced his goal to conquer Africa from "Cape to Cairo." He said he would paint Africa red from "C to C." He was willing to fight anyone who got in his way. And he succeeded.

In 1890, Rhodes became dissatisfied with his victories. He wanted not merely to occupy the land that is now Zimbabwe; he also wanted legal claim to it, which meant legal rights over the people. King Lobengula now understood Cecil Rhodes threatened the way of life of his people. So in 1891 he gave Lippert, a German, legal rights to the land that Rhodes occupied. Lippert had promised Lobengula that he would drive the British away. Instead Lippert immediately handed over his land rights to Rhodes. By December 1893, Cecil Rhodes had the land he wanted, and he named it "Rhodesia." For the indigenous people, the struggle had just begun.

I am almost at the top of the hill, the others are already there, but I am not ready yet. I leave the path and begin to journey around the perimeter of the hill. The wind blows stronger, and my skirt whips against my legs as I walk. I draw my raincoat closer to my body. The air is moist, and there is a chill I have not felt before in Zimbabwe. The dry grass snaps and flattens as my feet hit the earth.

Once Rhodes had conquered the land, the next task was to relocate the indigenous people. The Europeans claimed the desirable land and pushed the native people, and their agriculturally based lifestyles, onto land that was not fertile and had little rainfall, a practice that would continue into the 1960s. An 1894 provision established that native people should be given enough land to meet their present needs and those of future generations. The whites debated how many future generations had to be considered. The Ndebele people were granted land in Rhodesia that was infested with Malaria-carrying mosquitoes and bad flies. The Ndebele refused to live there.

A feudal system of government was introduced for the people who refused to move off their land into reservations. The Africans were forced to be servants to the whites and had no rights. Many African cultural practices were abolished. Legal segregation according to race and ethnicity was also established in 1894.

The indigenous peoples were forced to pay taxes in cash. But they had no cash, only cattle and livestock that the British would not accept in payment. So the Africans who had been self-sufficient for all of time now had to go to work for whites in order to earn cash for taxes. With men working for the British instead of for their families, the family structure had to change. When the Shona people protested, brutality followed. The whites seized Shona cattle and sold them for cash. The whites seized the wealth of the Shona and disrupted cultural practices that depended on the trade of cattle and other livestock.

Shona herds were not vaccinated like European cattle, because the Shona could not pay for the vaccine. Therefore, any cow that strayed from a Shona herd was shot, and the owner of the cow was not compensated in any way.

When there was a drought in 1896, the Ndebele and Shona took it as a sign that the gods were angry that the whites were there. They decided they must drive them out. War began and then ended when the British came in. They determined Rhodesia to be a white man's land. The blacks were to work on the land in the interest of the whites. Social, political, and economic relationships were structured to support that interest. It was not until 1980 that the indigenous people, the people who began here, were able to regain legal control over their land.

I feel that this land was once sacred. Before I came to this hill, I learned that this place had been sacred to the people who dwelled in the area. This land held the beliefs, the faith of the people. And today, standing on this sacred land, I feel the energy from a people who believed in it, who had a powerful faith. My legs grow stronger and stronger as they lead me toward the peak of the hill. My pace quickens against the violent wind that takes my words away to silence as I say aloud, "This is where Cecil John Rhodes is buried."

He took everything he could away from the people. He knew that this was a sacred place and it was here that he chose to be buried. He saw Africa and believed the land was his for the taking. Nothing in me can comprehend why the Europeans did not see the humanity of the African people. When Rhodes saw the people, he believed they were worth nothing, deserved nothing. I have lived now with the people of Zimbabwe. I have received the gifts of their culture and of their vitality. Each smile of a stranger in the city of Harare is a symbol of their humanity. Some things Rhodes could not take, could not own, could not destroy.

Still, I cannot escape the reality that twists brutally in my gut: he won. He won not only a fight for land and rule; he won the devastation of something special that could never be recreated. When Cecil Rhodes claimed his victory, the systems of belief and the faith that had made this land sacred were subordinated forever to the white man's culture, the white man's interest. This land cannot be the sacred place it once was now that this man, symbol of ignorance and destruction, claims it even in his death. And Zimbabwe, though an independent nation, is still subordinated in the international community. The racism and the cultural imperialism that the European explorers brought to Africa made a mark as permanent as death.

The cloud that began on the horizon is moving boldly, swiftly toward this place. The cloud is dark purple and blue and lightning slashes through it. Cecil John Rhodes's remains lie near me. And in this sacred place the sky seems angry, fighting to communicate the power of this place, the importance of what was lost. The flashing bolts of energy ignite the approaching darkness. Even in silence, the lightning speaks of an untouchable power.

I desperately want to walk on Rhodes's grave, to stomp on it, kick it, scream my rage at it. He has no right to be here. He never had any right to be here. I am the last person to leave. The others walk somberly down the hill as the driving rain pounds into every crevice of the earth. I turn to leave. And then I turn back. Herein lies Cecil Rhodes. I lift one leg and stomp down hard on the plaque that is now darkened with wetness. The hard surface jars my leg. I wait as the jarring subsides. Then I turn and walk down the hill. The thundering in the sky echoes in my head, and all I can think of is the lightning.

# V  Reflecting

For the first time in a while, all eighteen students in my group are together. We are at Lake Chivero for the evaluation period of our program. I think this period is supposed to feel like "closure" for us. Although I enjoy spending time with friends in the group and Lake Chivero is a quiet and beautiful place, I do not expect to find closure here. I expect to find it a long time from now. I imagine a moment when I am alone, with my memories, and thoughts spread before me. When I can see them all and gather them together to put away, I will have closure.

I am sitting on a rock on the edge of the lake. The air is still, and I breathe softly, mirroring the slight motion of the water at my feet. I like being alone and quiet. In Zimbabwe, I have learned to be alone.

At times, it has taken a lot of energy. Because I have had no one to process experiences with, I have had to find my own ways to make peace with difficult situations. Although it has sometimes been hard to have no one with whom to share my thoughts and feelings, the experience has taught me about acceptance. Not having anyone to validate my point of view has made me question my perspectives and open my mind to new ones.

I remember that at the beginning, when Baba Mandaza would make a sexist remark, I would instantly fill with anger and revulsion. Partly because there was no one to agree with me that his comment was despicable and partly because I was a guest both in his home and in his culture, I had to examine the whole situation on a deeper level. As a result, I did a lot of thinking and learning about the Shona culture and society, along with Baba Mandaza's position in it. Now I do not feel angry at him. I understand the roots of his beliefs.

Because the fact of sexism has never ceased to make me angry, I have felt driven to explore the position of women in Zimbabwe and how women here are addressing sexism. My capacity for anger at injustice has not lessened. But my acceptance of the roots of injustice has continued to broaden, and I have found ways to fuse my anger and acceptance. I think of my project on baby dumping as a culmination of this "teamwork."

Throughout my time here, I have felt myself separating from the person I was in the U.S., a separation I've seen most concretely in the letters I've written to friends in which I tried to describe everything. Early on, it became clear that I could not describe everything and that no one would be able to truly relate to my experience.

Sometimes I have felt torn between wanting to go back to the time when almost everyone I knew understood my life experiences, and wanting to go forward to see what else was out there to learn. The ambivalence was fleeting because of the strength of my desire to explore. The friends I have relied on through letters are the ones who grasp that this experience for me is bigger than we know. I remember writing to one friend, "If you get one thing from this letter, please just understand that this experience is what I have been waiting for."

My expectations of how a friend can know and understand me have changed. I had always felt that my closest friends and I could know each other almost as well as we knew ourselves. Now I see our separateness. Even when I first acknowledged these thoughts, I felt fine being separate. I think that on some level, I had understood from the beginning that this would be my time alone.

A young boy with a fishing pole walks by. I wonder if I have taken his rock, but a minute later I see him walk into the shallow water and climb onto a rock a few feet out. Once he sets up his line, he sits as still as I, as still as the air. His faded red shirt interrupts the wash of gray-blue sky and water.

In Zimbabwe, I have also become accustomed to being motionless. Being motionless usually feels good, as when I sat with Amai Kyandere on the kitchen hut floor waiting for the water to boil. Sometimes even waiting for a bus that may never come can feel good. It has to do with acceptance, allowing for a slower pace, and understanding that nothing is really predictable.

It is almost time for me to return to the United States. In a few days, I will sit on the edge of the bed in the room I grew up in. Will I remember how I feel in this moment at Lake Chivero? I look down at the water to see my reflection, but there isn't one. All I can see from this rock is who I am inside. I smile because I know that this reflection will not change.

I am walking up metal stairs to the large airplane with the engine that rumbles like an earthquake. The whiteness of the airplane cuts into the bright blue sky, and I can smell the pavement in the hot sun. Hannah was supposed to meet me at Ranche House College and come here with me. My cab arrived early and I had to leave without her. As sad as I am to not see her one last time, I cannot feel too distressed; rigid schedules never work in Zimbabwe. I had to be here to catch the plane. My belongings are zipped into duffel bags. A sweatshirt that I never wore here is wrapped around my waist. It might be cold on the plane.

I am no longer in Zimbabwe. I am nowhere, really, just in the air. I see South Africa below me. I can see mines and some roads, but I cannot see people. It is strange that no matter how fast the plane moves through the air, everything inside the plane stays perfectly still. The place I have just left had been unknown to me. The place I am going had been familiar to me. It is strange that though my body sits perfectly still, my thoughts run fast, like a river, through my mind.

Inside of me there are new voices and new eyes. I hear the songs of Wachikwa. I see Hannah's eyes as she reads about women in the liberation struggle and in the moment before she tells me that Marcus hit her in the face. I hear Amai Mamutse talking with a destitute woman who holds a three-month-old baby. I see Amai Mamutse's home and the plate she has given me laden with potatoes and sadza. I see Amai Kyandere's face as she walks with me to my first day at Kyandere Primary. I hear Baba's voice responding to my greeting as I look up at him from my kneeling position. I see Hannah as she smiles at me and gives me my Shona name. The voices inside me speak as one: "Tonderai," they say. Remember.